VISUAL THINKING

Marco Meirovitz
Paul I. Jacobs

TRILLIUM PRESS
New York

Trillium Press, Inc.
PO Box 209
Monroe, New York 10950
(914) 783-2999

Printed in the United States of America
ISBN: 0-89824-184-7

Phototypeset for highest quality by Trillium Services, Inc.

TABLE OF CONTENTS

Improve Thinking Skills Through Games

The Need

Our ability to think is more important today than twenty, ten or even five years ago. We face more complex challenges in our daily lives from computers, two-way television, automatic banking and other technological developments than we ever did before. We must improve our abilities to think in systematic, efficient and creative ways in order just to cope.

The Answer

The present book—to teach visual thinking—is part of a larger international project, the Muscles of the Mind Program for helping people realize their intellectual potential.

The Muscles of the Mind Program for teaching thinking skills in both homes and schools, developed by Marco Meirovitz, has been tried out and refined in Australia, France, Germany, Israel, Japan, and the United States.

The Muscles of the Mind Program uses games, puzzles and other activities designed to be fun so that learners from age 8 up to 80 can play, enjoy and benefit from them without specific prior knowledge.

The program provides a variety of activities to develop and exercise the major thinking skills. It provides practice in applying these skills to a wide variety of everyday life situations. You are also encouraged to apply this interdisciplinary program to all your school subjects, and various professional and vocational activities.

We know that some people learn better with visual materials, others with abstract materials, still other with verbal materials, etc. The complete program provides something for every kind of learner.

Brain Muscle Builders, the first book based upon the Muscles of the Mind Program, deals with games of abstract thinking. This book is now available in many languages (French: *Le Jogging de L'Esprit*; German: *Spielschule Des Denkens*, Spanish: *Desafe A Su Inteligencia*; etc.).

Now *Visual Thinking*, the second book, is available for exercising and improving visual thinking skills. It deals with Logic, Strategy, Memory, Creativity, Problem-Solving, etc., making use of such interesting materials as mosaics, puzzles, tangrams, polyominoes, and mazes.

The Aim of this Book

This book shows you how to improve your visual thinking. It deals with the general *abstract* thinking skills of deductive logic, inductive logic, strategy, and memory in a visual context, and with more *specific* visual thinking skills, such as observation, visualization, and imagining changes in visual situations.

The book allows you to play unlimited numbers of games in which you use most of your intellectual potential. You learn new techniques for using the visual thinking skills in the most efficient way. The book also gives you the right habits of thinking and shows how to apply principles from the games you play to solve everyday problems. For example, by playing games of deductive logic (see Chapter 10) you practice and get used to the skill of deduction by elimination. This technique is used to solve practical problems by a doctor in diagnosing a patient's malady, by a car mechanic in finding the malfunction in a car, and by a TV repairperson in repairing a television set.

The book also shows you how to apply what you've learned about visual thinking to practical problems.

Organization of the Book

This book contains 13 chapters of games and puzzles, each dealing with a particular topic. Each chapter contains:
- an introduction to the topic: what it is and why it is important;
- activities to get you familiar with the topic;
- puzzles and games for you to play by yourself, and in some cases, with others;
- answers to the puzzles at the end of the chapter.

A final chapter invites you to apply what you have learned from one or more chapters to a set of practical problems.

The games and puzzles in each chapter are often arranged in groups. Within groups, they are roughly arranged in order of difficulty, from easiest to hardest.

How To Use the Book

In general you can read and use each chapter by itself. In some cases we refer you to material in an earlier chapter when this will help you prepare for what you are working on.

Always start with the first game in a group. This game is analyzed for you, its rules are the most thoroughly discussed, and sample games are provided. If you find that the first game in a group is not challenging enough for you, you can then skip ahead to a later game in the same group. When you find the right level for yourself within a group of games, stay with it until you have mastered it. Then move on.

As you can see, the book is more like a handbook than one you would read straight through only once from beginning to end. You can go through it many times, enjoying and learning from it each time. The book can provide many merry hours of fun for everyone in the family, children and grownups alike. You may therefore want to dip into the book on many different occasions: on a train or plane ride, when sick, when friends drop in, to make new friends, to entertain old friends, when you're looking for an activity to break the ice at a gathering where people don't know each other well, and so on.

Some of the activities are puzzles, not games. A puzzle has one route to the solution. In a game, however, a different set of events may occur each time it's played, even with the same rules.

You can play many of the games by yourself. Other games can be played with two or more players. After you play a game with others, discuss it with them. As you enter the minds of other people and see how they think, you can improve your own thinking and playing.

What You Need To Play

For most of the activities, puzzles and games in the book you need:

- 96 mosaic pieces. Each piece is square in shape, and has one of these six designs:

■	◧	◪	▨	✕
32	24	24	8	8

The number tells how many there are of the piece above it.

- 14 monomino pieces, each square in shape, and one fourth the size of a mosaic piece
- 6 domino pieces, each equal in area to two monomino pieces

- 10 tromino pieces, each equal in area to three monomino pieces

- 20 tetraminoes, each equal in area to four monomino pieces

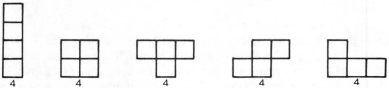

- 24 pentominoes, each equal in area to five monomino pieces

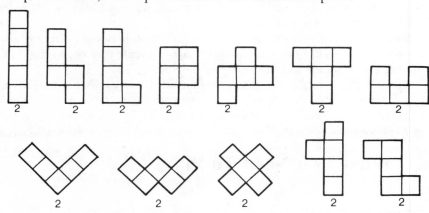

- 2 sets of "tangram" pieces. Each set looks like this:

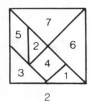

For a few of the activities you may also need such common objects as scissors, a ruler, a pencil, paper, graph paper, matches, and a few coins.

- A board or "grid" divided into eight rows of eight boxes each.

Each box should be large enough to contain one mosaic piece. Label each left-to-right row in the grid 1, 2, 3...8. Label each top-to-bottom column A, B, C...H. These numbers and letters are the *coordinates,* which we use to refer to particular squares. For example, in Fig. 1 an "X" appears in square B5.

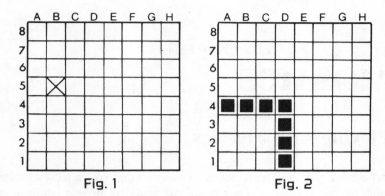

Fig. 1   Fig. 2

Each game we present has a *"Materials Needed"* section. It tells you the size of any grid you may need to draw for a particular game. In some games, you will use the entire 8x8 grid. In other games, you will use only part of it, such as a 3x3 grid. When you need a grid smaller than 8x8, mark off the boundaries of the grid with the pieces you won't need in that particular game. Fig. 2 shows a 3x3 grid marked off with black mosaic pieces.

When you mark off a grid smaller than 8x8, always start at the lower left-hand corner (square A1). Then the coordinates of the area you use will always match the coordinates in our description and analysis of the game.

Some games require a "grid of dots." For these games, use a piece of ordinary graph paper. Place dots where the lines meet. Fig. 34 shows a section of graph paper that has been turned into a 4x4 "grid of dots."

Fig. 3

CHAPTER I

MOSAICS

Playing with Mosaics

In this chapter you will learn about mosaics so that you can create designs, draw pictures, and improve your power to visualize how a whole is made up of its parts, and to build a whole from parts. First, we will describe the tiles from the kit you can use to build mosaics, then we will define some terms, give you some activities to become familiar with mosaics, present some mosaic puzzles for you to solve, describe some mosaic games you can play by yourself or with others, tell you how to build some new sets of mosaic tiles, and finally, show you how to create designs and draw pictures with mosaics.

The tiles

You have a set of tiles like these: ■ ▯ ◩
What happens when you turn them clockwise by 90 degrees four times? Let's look first at ◩ . We will first put numbers on each corner. On the first turn 90 degrees clockwise, the "1" goes from upper left to upper right. The tile is divided by a diagonal line running from "2" to "4," and is blackened from that line to corner "3."

a) ■ is the same in all four positions
b) ▯ is different in each of the four possible positions:

1
    ▯   ▭   ▯   ▭
    2   3   4   5

c) ◩ is different in each of the four possible positions:

    ◣   ◥   ◤   ◢
    6   7   8   9

d) When you leave a square on the grid blank, you have ☐ . In effect, then, you have 10 different tiles.

10

Mosaics

A *mosaic* is a group of tiles arranged to form a picture or design by connecting them along their edges so that the corners coincide, as shown in Fig. 1a:

A mosaic
Fig. 1a

Not a mosaic:
Fig. 1b

Not a mosaic:
Fig. 1c

Figs. 1b and 1c are *not* mosaics. In Fig. 1b the edges are not all connected, and in Fig. 1c all the corners don't coincide.

First we will consider mosaics made up of 8 tiles placed 4 across and 2 tiles down, as shown in Fig. 1a. We will call this a *4x2* mosaic.

Symmetry

There are two different kinds of mosaics, *symmetric* and *nonsymmetric*.

A *symmetric* mosaic can be divided into two halves that are "mirror images" of each other. This means that when you place half a mosaic on a mirror, you actually see the entire mosaic. An example is shown in Fig. 2.

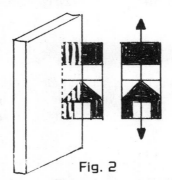

Fig. 2

If you don't have a mirror, you can always fold a symmetric mosaic so that the two halves coincide exactly, as shown in Fig. 3.

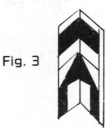

Fig. 3

A *nonsymmetrical* mosaic *cannot* be divided into halves that are mirror images of each other, and when folded into halves, they do not coincide.

Fig. 4 shows some examples of symmetric and nonsymmetric mosaics. Note that for some symmetric mosaics you can place the mirror (or fold the paper) in more than one place.

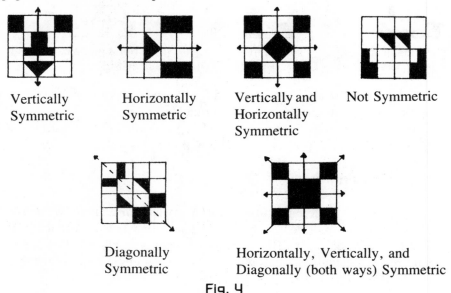

Vertically Symmetric

Horizontally Symmetric

Vertically and Horizontally Symmetric

Not Symmetric

Diagonally Symmetric

Horizontally, Vertically, and Diagonally (both ways) Symmetric

Fig. 4

Rotation

You can systematically change any mosaic by rotation of the whole mosaic grid. We have already seen that you can rotate a single tile into four different positions with horizontal and vertical edges. You can do the same thing with a mosaic, as seen in Fig. 5:

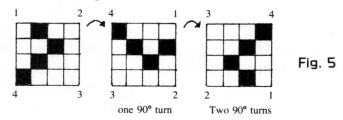

one 90° turn

Two 90° turns

Fig. 5

But you cannot change a symmetrical mosaic into a nonsymmetrical mosaic (or vice versa) by rotation.

Black/white reversal

You can reverse a mosaic made up of two different colors, such as black and white, by making the black areas white and the white areas black, as shown in Fig. 6:

Fig. 6

But you cannot change a symmetrical mosaic into a nonsymmetrical mosaic (or vice versa) by black/white reversal.

ACTIVITIES

Now that you know what we mean by *symmetric* and *nonsymmetric mosaics, rotation* and *black/white reversal,* let's do some activities in which you use these powerful ideas.

Symmetry

In this first set of activities, build as many *different* symmetric mosaics as you can.

We say two mosaics are different when you cannot change one into the other by rotation or by reversing black and white. From this point of view, all the mosaics in Figs. (5) and (6) are the same.

Build as many different symmetric mosaics as you can, using:
1) 18 each of □ and ■ tiles (mosaic size 6x6)
2) 12 each of □, ■, and ◪ tiles (mosaic size 6x6)
3) 9 each of □, ■, ◪, and ◩ tiles (mosaic size 6x6)
4) 12 each of □ and ■ and 20 each of ◪ and ◩ tiles (mosaic size 8x8).

Check that each mosaic you build *is* symmetric:
a. Separate the tiles of the mosaic slightly into what you think are two mirror image halves (Fig. 7a,b).
b. Use some new tiles to make a copy of one half of the mosaic.
c. Lay a mirror on the table. Place the copy on it (Fig. 7c).
d. If the copy and its image together look exactly like your original mosaic, then your original mosaic is symmetric. If they look different, then it is not. The circles show where they look different.

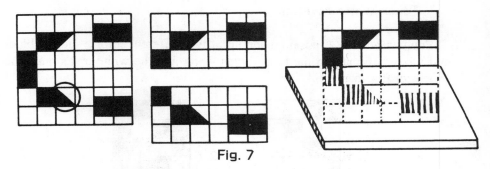

Fig. 7

A System for Building Symmetric Mosaics

Did you have any trouble building a symmetric mosaic? Here's a systematic way to build one. Suppose you want to build a *horizontally* symmetric 6x6 mosaic.

1. Place any tile anywhere on a 6x6 grid, as in Fig. 8a.
2. Imagine the grid is divided into two sections by a mirror.
3. Place a second tile in the other section so that it looks like the first tile reflected in the mirror, as in Fig. 8b.
   a) Both tiles will be the same distance from the mirror, but on opposite sides.
   b) A solid color tile gets reflected to the same solid color; A tile that is not a solid color gets reflected with its colors reversed from left to right, or top to bottom. See Fig. 8c.

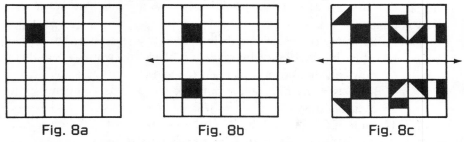

| Fig. 8a | Fig. 8b | Fig. 8c |

Continue in this way, placing a tile and then its reflection, and you will build up a symmetric mosaic.

Here's a hint to remember how to "reflect" a tile: Think of the grid as hinged in the middle. Flip the left side over, as in Fig. 9.

Fig. 9

You can use this same systematic way to build a mosaic that is:
— vertically symmetric (Fig. 10a)
— diagonally symmetric (Fig. 10b)
— horizontally and vertically symmetric (Fig. 10c)
— diagonally symmetric both ways (Fig. 10d).

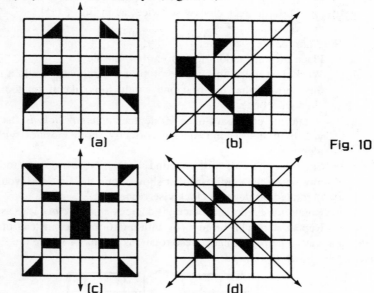

Fig. 10

In the last two cases, imagine the grid divided into four sections by two mirrors.

With diagonally symmetric mosaics, some tiles will be placed half on one side of the mirror, and half on the other. Note that a ◣ tile can only be placed across the mirror as shown in Fig. 11a, and not as in Fig. 11b.

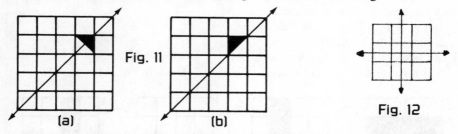

Fig. 11

Fig. 12

Up to now we have been using grids with an *even* number of rows and columns, for example, 6x6. In these cases the horizontal and vertical lines of symmetry run along the edges of the boxes. But when a grid has an *odd* number of rows and columns, for example, 3x3 as in Fig. 12, then the horizontal and vertical lines of symmetry cut through the boxes, as they do in all cases with diagonal lines of symmetry.

Rotation

In this next set of activities, first create a mosaic, and then, using other tiles, build copies of that mosaic
  (a)   turned 90 degrees clockwise once, and
  (b)   turned 90 degrees clockwise twice, as in Fig. 5

Here are the steps to take:
  a.   Place tiles at random to form a 4x4 mosaic.
  b.   Work next with other tiles on top of a cardboard. Build a new mosaic that shows what the first one would look like if rotated 90 degrees clockwise once.
  c.   Rotate the cardboard once 90 degrees *counterclockwise* as a check. If you built the second mosaic correctly, both mosaics will now look identical.
  d.   Scramble the tiles of the second mosaic. Now use them to build a new mosaic on the cardboard that shows what the first one would look like if rotated 90 degrees clockwise twice.
  e.   Rotate the cardboard twice 90 degrees *counterclockwise* as a check.
  f.   Repeat steps (1) through (6) with a 6x6 mosaic, instead of a 4x4.

Here's a way to help you make these rotations: Think of where the first row will move to, as shown in Fig. 13:

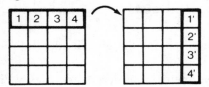

Fig. 13

Tile 1 will move to position 1', tile 2 to position 2', etc. A solid color tile will look the same in its new location.

But a ◨ tile will look like this: ⬓
a ⬓ tile will look like this: ◨
a ◣ tile will look like this: ◥, etc.

The other three rows will move to the places shown in Fig. 14.

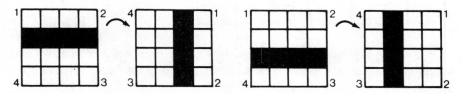

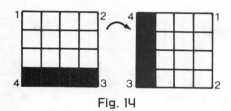

Fig. 14

Puzzles

Now that you have been through some activities to get used to mosaics, here are some mosaic puzzles to work on. In each case the answers are at the end of the chapter.

I.   Which of these are symmetric?

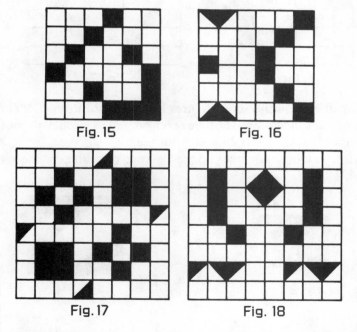

Fig. 15   Fig. 16

Fig. 17   Fig. 18

II.   What will each of these look like when turned 90 degrees clockwise? Construct it with your tiles, without turning the book.

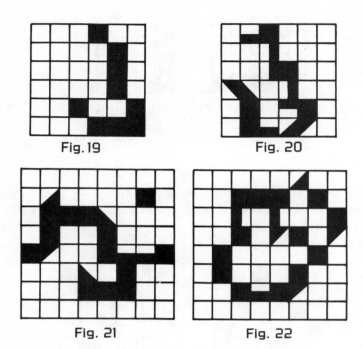

Fig. 19   Fig. 20

Fig. 21   Fig. 22

III. What will each of the above figures look like when turned 90 degrees clockwise *and* black and white are reversed? Construct it with your tiles.
IV. Construct Figures 23 to 28 with your tiles.
V. Practice building from mosaic pieces your own shapes like those in Figs. 23 to 28.

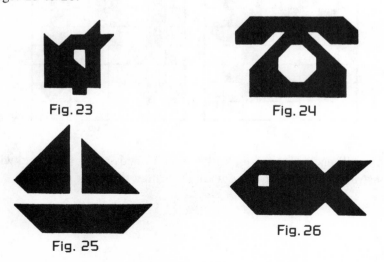

Fig. 23   Fig. 24

Fig. 25   Fig. 26

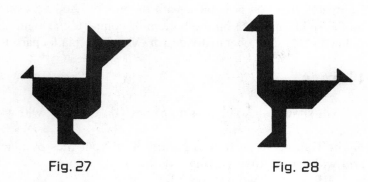

Fig. 27   Fig. 28

The way to build Figs. 23 to 28 is similar to how you would put dominoes together, but you build in all four directions, instead of just in a line. Begin either from the middle or a corner of the shape.

For example, here's a systematic way to build Fig. 23.

Look first at the upper left hand part of the figure.

a.   Get a ◣ by placing a ◥

b.   Get a ◢ by adding ◪ on the right. ◖◗

c.   Add black tiles beneath to reach

d.   Add a black tile to the upper right, and imagine a white tile below it.

e.   Add a ◥ below the white tile.

f.   Now add three tiles below the last tile you placed and four more black tiles on the right to get:

g.   Compare what you now have with the model. Add a ◼ on top, a ◪ on the right, and a ◪ on the bottom to complete the figure.

In general, remember to divide a drawing into smaller parts to copy it.

Games

Now we will show you some mosaic games you can play with your tiles:

*MOS 1.

Aim of the Game: To be first to get rid of all your tiles by placing them on a grid without destroying symmetry.

Number of Players: Two or more.

Materials Needed: All 96 mosaic tiles; 6x6 grid.

How to Play: Each player is given 10 tiles at random. The remaining tiles are placed face down on the table as a "bank." The first player places any one of his/her tiles on any square of the grid. Each player in turn places one of his/her tiles on any square on the grid, as long as it does not destroy the horizontal or vertical symmetry of the tiles already placed. A player who cannot place a tile must draw one from the bank. The tile drawn may not be placed until the player's next turn.

The first player to get rid of all his/her tiles wins.

Variation: Use 8x8 grid; each player gets 16 tiles.

In Fig. 29, only a ◪ can be placed in B2 (to maintain horizontal symmetry); only a ◤ can be placed in E5 (to maintain vertical symmetry); only a ◼ can be placed in C5 (to maintain vertical symmetry), etc.

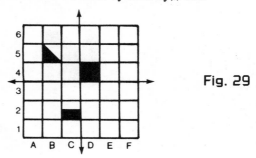

Fig. 29

In the next game, too, each player tries to be first to get rid of all his/her tiles. The players must recognize how a mosaic has been built, and build a copy, according to some rules.

*MOS 2.

Aim of the Game: To get rid of your tiles by building a copy of a mosaic.

Number of Players: Two or more.

Materials Needed: All 96 mosaic tiles; 5x5 grid.

How to Play: One player builds a 5x5 mosaic as a model left in view of all players. Along each edge where two tiles meet, two black areas or two white areas must share a border.

Five tiles are dealt out to each player. Each player keeps his/her tiles from the view of the other players.

Players alternate turns, placing one of their tiles on the table. Each tile placed after the first must (a) contribute to building an exact copy of the model, and (b) share a common edge with a tile already placed.

The player placing the first tile must state where on the model it fits. A player who cannot place a tile on the grid loses a turn. The first player to get rid of all his/her tiles is the winner. If no player can place a tile, the player with *fewest* tiles left wins.

Variation: Player builds 8x8 mosaic instead of 5x5; ten tiles are dealt out to each player instead of five.

Variation: The first tile placed must be the central tile of the mosaic. Each later tile must share a common edge with the one just placed, and must continue a spiral pattern, clockwise or counterclockwise (see Fig. 30).

Fig. 30 Example of Clockwise Spiral

Let's go over a game together. Fig. 31a shows the model, along with Player A and B's starting tiles.

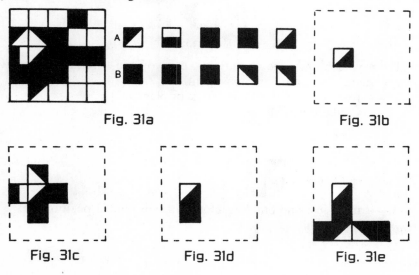

Fig. 31a

Fig. 31b

Fig. 31c

Fig. 31d

Fig. 31e

Player A starts with a tile in the position shown in Fig. 31b. Player A has made this choice because each of A's other tiles could on later moves be placed next to the tile A has just placed (Fig. 31c).

Player B then places a tile as shown in Fig. 31d. B hopes on later turns to place B's other tiles as shown in Fig. 31e.

Both players, then, think ahead in choosing a tile to place. They try to create opportunities to place their other tiles on later moves. In general, the strategy is like in the game of dominoes: keep some of each kind; get rid of those you have the most of.

Patterns, Designs and Pictures with Mosaics

You can apply what you've learned about mosaics to creating designs, and to drawing pictures. Let's see how.

Creating Designs

Get ready now to use what you already know about symmetry, rotation, and black/white reversal to create designs.

1.   Look at the design in Fig. 32.

Fig. 32

From your knowledge of mosaics, can you see several different ways it was created? Here are some possibilities:

— from just one building block or element,
— like this:
— or this:

— or this:

— from just one building block, in two rotated positions,
— like this:

— or this:

2.   How is the design in Fig. 33 made up?

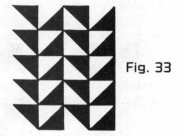

Fig. 33

You could see it as
— one elementary building block in two positions:

— one block in one position: or

3.   Fig. 34 shows how you can produce an illusion of depth with a square tile:

Fig. 34

4.   You can also make mosaics with curved lines. The design in Fig. 35 is made from a single building block with curved lines, and a black/ white reversal of it.

Fig. 35

Let's see some ways you can create complicated designs *without* using complicated building blocks.

5.   Begin with a 4x4 mosaic (Fig. 37a), rotate it into all four positions, and bring them together to form a 16x16 mosaic (Fig. 37b).

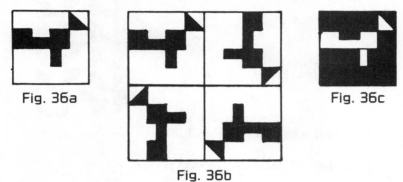

Fig. 36a   Fig. 36c

Fig. 36b

6.   Create a black/white reversed version of it (Fig. 37c), and use the two versions together to build larger designs.

Drawing pictures

You can use the four basic tiles (in ten positions) as the building blocks to "draw" pictures of objects such as a person kicking a ball (Fig. 37a), a dog (Fig. 37b), and a car (Fig. 37c).

1.   "Draw" a picture of a telephone, using mosaic tiles.
2.   "Draw" a picture of a ship, using mosaic tiles.

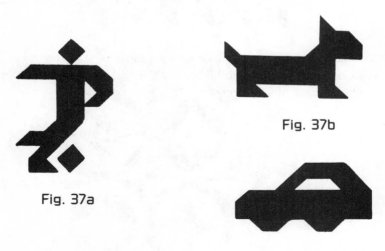

Fig. 37b

Fig. 37a

Fig. 37c

SOLUTIONS

Page 13

Fig. 15 Symmetric
Fig. 16 Symmetric
Fig. 17 Not Symmetric
Fig. 18 Not Symmetric

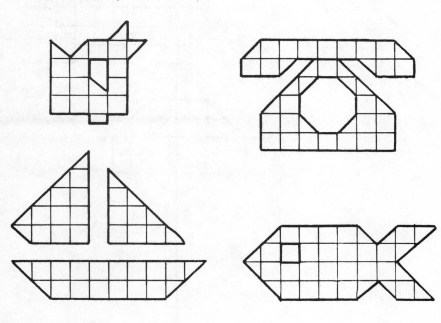

Page 14

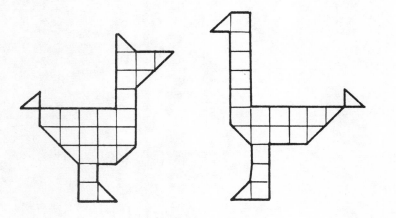

Page 20

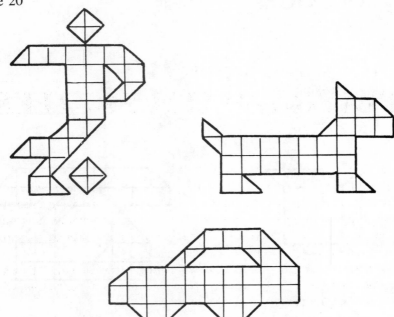

CHAPTER II

PLAYING WITH PUZZLES

As a child you may have worked on jigsaw puzzles. You were given differently shaped pieces with complicated markings, that were cut from a picture you had to restore. Sometimes you were shown what the completed **puzzle looked like.** If you weren't (or if you lost the cover of the box!), **then you found** the puzzle much harder to do.

The general idea of a puzzle is to find how different small pieces of information fit together. A detective story is a kind of puzzle, in which some pieces of information are verbal:

— "I was playing cards with some friends when I heard a shot."
— "I saw a tall man run out of the building."

Some pieces of information are visual:

— footprints near the scene of the crime.
— a broken window.

and some are more abstract ideas:

— the motive
— opportunities.

A jigsaw puzzle is like a detective story in which the pieces of information are given *visually*. For example,

— a red line on one puzzle piece may continue on another piece.
— a shoe on one puzzle piece must match a leg on another piece.
— of a tree, table, house, etc., must match the other part(s) on other piece(s).

But the visual skills you improve by playing with puzzles may be helpful to you, as we shall see, in a wider range of situations, with verbal, visual and more abstract pieces of information.

In this chapter we will give you experience first in restoring a cut-up picture, then restoring a cut-up shape without a picture, then show you how to build and play with your own puzzles, and finally give you some puzzle exercises to work out on your own.

We begin with a game you can play by yourself or with others.

Games

*PUZ 1.

Aim of the Game: To restore the pieces of a cut-up picture.

Number of Players: One or more.

Materials Needed: Newspaper or magazine, scissors, ruler, pencil.

How to Play:

I.   For one player

    a.   Locate a newspaper or magazine photograph.

       A complicated situation (several people, houses, cars, a street scene, etc.) or a caricature of a person will provide more challenge than a simple photo of a person's head.

    b.   Turn the photo on to its reverse side, and divide it with straight lines into 8 approximately equal vertical strips.

    c.   Number these strips "1" to "8" from left to right, then cut them out.

    d.   Scramble them, then turn the strips right side up.

    e.   Restore the pieces into the original photograph (Fig. 1).

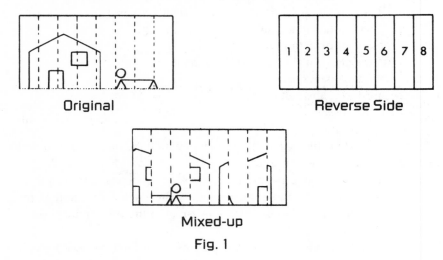

Original   Reverse Side

Mixed-up

Fig. 1

The numbers have three purposes:

— If you are stuck, peek at the number on the back of a strip.

— If you complete the puzzle but are not sure you have done it correctly, use the numbers to check.

— The numbers also help you detect if a piece is accidentally flipped over on to its other side.

II.   For more than one player

Each player locates, divides, numbers and cuts up a different photograph, and hands the pieces to the player on the right. No peeking at numbers is allowed. The first to correctly restore a photograph wins.

Variation: Cut the photograph into 10 to 20 vertical strips (your choice of how many).

Variation: Cut the photograph into 10 to 20 *horizontal* strips (your choice of how many). Number them from top to bottom, instead of from left to right.

Variation: Divide the photograph into 4 vertical strips, and then divide each strip into 4 horizontal strips. Number the pieces from left to right in the top row, from left to right in the next row, etc. (Fig. 2).

Variation: Make diagonal cuts only. Make 8 or more pieces.

Variation: Make diagonal, vertical and horizontal cuts to form 6 or more irregular pieces whose sides are not parallel. Each piece should be different from the others.

Variation: Make curved cuts only to form 6 or more pieces.

1	2	3	4
5	6	7	8
9	10	11	12
13	14	15	16

Fig. 2

When you play this game and its variations, concentrate on how the picture continues from piece to piece. Do not concentrate on the shapes of the pieces themselves. For example, in Fig. 3, if part of the house is missing, look for the piece that contains the rest of the house.

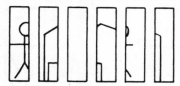

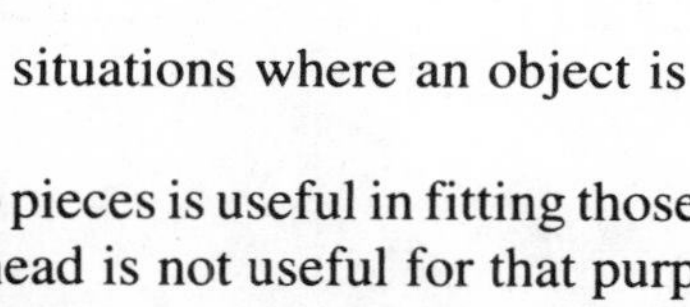

Fig. 3 Which piece will continue the house?

In general, look for situations where an object is partly on one piece and partly on another:

— A head in two pieces is useful in fitting those two pieces together.

— A complete head is not useful for that purpose, but could be useful for fitting its piece to the piece with the neck and shoulders.

As you improve in each variation, add more pieces.

If you have access to a photocopying machine, you can copy a photograph before you cut it up. Then you play the game in two ways:

— you are allowed to look at the photocopy while putting the pieces together

— you are not allowed to look at the photocopy.

In the last puzzle game you had to restore a "picture" by paying attention to what was drawn on each piece. In the next game you must restore a square that has been cut up by paying attention to the *shapes* of the pieces.

*PUZ 2.

Aim of the Game: To restore the pieces of a cut-up square.

Number of Players: One or more.

Materials Needed: Paper, pencil, scissors.

How to Play:

I.   For one player

1.   Cut a 6″ or larger square of paper into 6 rectangular pieces (Fig. 4).

2.   Mix them up.

3.   Restore the original square.

II.   For more than one player

Each player cuts up a different square, and hands the pieces to the player on the right. The first to restore a square wins.

Variation: Cut the square into 8 to 12 rectangles.

Variation: Cut the square into 4 to 7 triangles (Fig. 5).

Variation: Cut the square into a mixture of 6 or more rectangles and triangles (Fig. 6).

Variation: Cut the square into a mixture of 6 or more irregular shapes (Fig. 7).

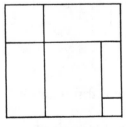

Fig. 4

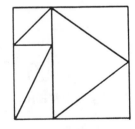

Fig. 5

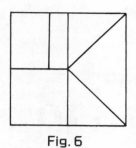

Fig. 6

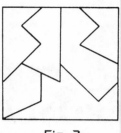

Fig. 7

Note that the more regular and alike you make the pieces, the harder the puzzle becomes. This is because many pieces will appear to fit together that don't really fit together in the completed puzzle. For example, in Fig. 8,

HI of piece 7 fits with
— EG of piece 6
— AE of piece 1
— BC of piece 5, etc.

Fig. 8

EH of piece 6 fits with
— FI of piece 7
— FI of piece 8
— CF of piece 5
— (AD of piece 1) + (DF of piece 3), etc.

Playing with these pieces gives you good practice in putting pieces together by concentrating on the shapes. Earlier we asked you to concentrate on the pictures of the pieces you assembled and to ignore the shapes of the pieces. Now pay attention to both shapes and pictures at the same time.

1.   Paste a picture from a newspaper or magazine onto a sheet of cardboard. Cut the cardboard into irregular pieces (as in Fig. 7, for example).
2.   Scramble the pieces.
3.   Restore the picture.

FROM PUZZLES TO TANGRAMS

The tangram game comes from China, and is at least hundreds of years old. The seven tangram pieces fit together to form a square. The basic idea of tangrams is to use all seven pieces to construct geometric shapes and pictures.

With puzzles, too, you put together pieces to form geometric shapes and pictures. But there are three major differences between tangrams and puzzles:

1. Tangrams use the same set of pieces in each activity. These pieces are shown in Fig. 1. We have numbered the pieces to make it easier to refer to them.

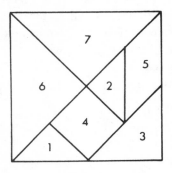

Fig. 1

2. Tangram pieces contain no markings or colorings: only the shape of each piece matters. To get some direct experience with these differences between tangrams and puzzles:

— Take a jigsaw puzzle, turn all the pieces over, and try to put the puzzle together. You will see what it is like to solve a puzzle when only the *shape* of the piece is important.

— Cut out a picture in the shapes of your tangram set.

— Scramble the pieces, and try to solve. You will see how easy it is. You will find later that the tangram pieces *without* pictures are not that easy to put together.

3. Almost any tangram piece can be connected to any other piece.

Activities

Squares from Two Kinds of Pieces

I. 1. Cut a 4x4 square grid into 8 pieces, as in Fig. 2. These 8 pieces are really two different sets of 4 pieces each, △ and ◸.

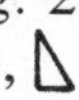

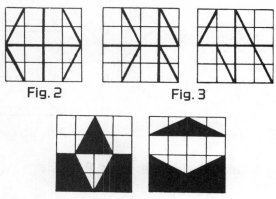

Fig. 2   Fig. 3

Fig. 4

  2. Mix these 8 pieces up.

  3. See how many different ways you can put them together again to form a square. Fig. 3 shows you some of the many possibilities.

II. 1. Make another set of 8 pieces like the first, but from a different colored paper.

  2. Mix the two sets together so that you have 16 pieces.

  3. Build interesting squares from 8 of these 16 pieces. Fig. 4 shows some possibilities.

You've seen what you can do with just two different shapes. Now let's see what you can do with the actual tangram pieces.

The Tangram Pieces

Your tangram kit consists of 7 pieces: 2 large triangles, 1 medium size triangle, 2 small triangles, a square, and a parallelogram. With these pieces you will see you can make many wonderful pictures and shapes. But first you must become familiar with the individual pieces and how they fit together.

The small triangle is the basic unit in the tangram set. You use it in making a copy of every other piece in the tangram set:

— By putting together 2 small triangles you can make the square, the medium size triangle, and the parallelogram (Fig 5a).

— And by putting the 2 small triangles together with either the square, the medium size triangle or the parallelogram, you can make the large triangle (Fig. 5b).

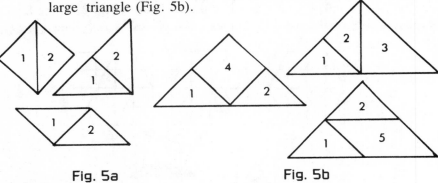

Fig. 5a   Fig. 5b

Building Squares with Tangram Pieces

Make a square from 2 or more tangram pieces. Do it several other ways before you read further.

Have you been able to build a square from 2, 3, 4, 5 and 7 tangram pieces? Let's look now at how it's done.

1.   The simplest way is to put two identical triangles together.

— Fig. 5 shows how two small triangles form a square.

— We can also use two large triangles, as in Fig. 6.

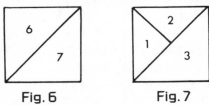

Fig. 6   Fig. 7

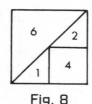

Fig. 8

2. We can't use two medium size triangles because we only have one. But wait: we can form another from two small triangles, and then put the two medium size triangles together, as in Fig. 7. In this way we use *three* tangram pieces.
3. We can also combine 4 pieces to make a square. We can use one large triangle plus a set of three pieces that together make up a large triangle, as in Fig. 8.
4. Now build squares from 5 and from 7 tangram pieces.

Building Rectangles with Tangram Pieces

Let's see how we can build rectangles with tangram pieces.
1. Build a rectangle from two small triangles and the square, as in Fig. 9a.
2. Build a rectangle from 2 small triangles and the medium size triangle, as in Fig. 9b.
3. Make the rectangle in Fig. 9a longer but with the same width:
    — Add the square at either end, as in Fig. 10.
    — Add the parallelogram between the medium triangle and one of the small triangles. You may need to flip over the parallelogram first, as in Fig. 11.

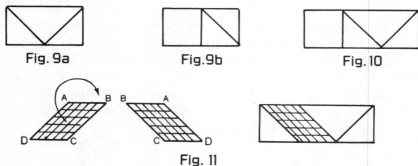

Fig. 9a   **Fig.9b**   **Fig. 10**

Fig. 11

Now that you know how to make squares and rectangles in many different ways, let's see some things we can do with them.

Building Tangram Pictures from Simple Geometric Shapes

1. Make one square from the two large triangles, and another, the same size, from the other 5 pieces. You could put the two squares side by side to form a rectangle, but try to find more interesting ways to combine them, as in Fig. 12.

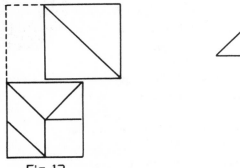

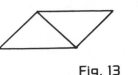

Fig. 13

Fig. 12

2. Make an interesting combination of two different size squares.
3. Remember that two identical triangles can be combined to form a parallelogram as well as a square (Fig. 13). Use the pieces from both tangram sets together. Make interesting combinations of:
    (a) squares and parallelograms
    (b) squares, triangles, and parallelograms
    (c) squares, triangles, parallelograms and rectangles.

Copying Tangram Figures

Now that you have some experience in building with squares, rectangles, triangles and parallelograms, let's turn to copying figures. Suppose you are given the outline of a figure that has been made with all 7 tangram pieces. Can you reconstruct how it was done? Let's see. Fig. 14 presents some outlines to try. The side of each piece does not need to line up exactly with the side of another piece. In the first and third figures of Fig. 14 you will find that some pieces touch only at a point.

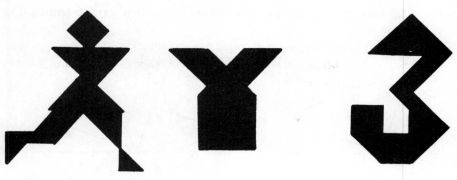

Fig. 14

Let's go over the first one, the boat, together. It looks like it has three basic parts, a left sail, a right sail, and a bottom.

— The left sail is simply a triangle (but we don't yet know which one or whether it's made up of smaller pieces).
— The right sail is also a triangle shape (but we don't know yet which one or whether it's made up of smaller pieces).
— The bottom is like a long rectangle, except that the ends are not squared off.

Let's try to build the bottom first.

1.   Build a long rectangle as you did earlier.

2.   See if you can modify it to make the ends look like the bottom section of the boat.

The key is to use a square instead of the medium size triangle, as in Fig. 15a. Place a small triangle on both sides of the square, to get the basic boat-bottom shape (Fig. 15b). Then add the parallelogram on either side to lengthen the boat-bottom (Fig. 15c).

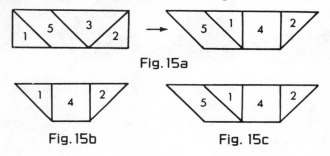

Fig. 15a

Fig. 15b   Fig. 15c

3. Make the middle section by combining the two large triangles (Fig. 15d).
4. Add the remaining small triangle for the top (Fig. 15e).

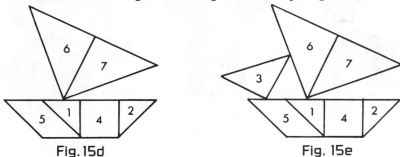

Fig. 15d   Fig. 15e

Solutions for the other four figures are given in the back of the chapter.

Some Tangram Puzzles to Solve

1. There are some shapes like that in Fig. 16 that you can make in two different ways:
    — using three of the tangram pieces, and
    — using the other four pieces.

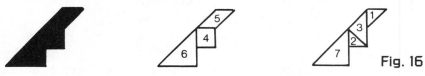

Fig. 16

Build each of the following figures in two ways, using first three of the seven tangram pieces, then using the other four.

2. There are also some figures you can make in two *almost* identical ways using all seven tangram pieces. The person in Fig. 17a has a foot, the person in Fig. 17b does not. Do you see how this is done? Build both Figs. 17a and 17b.

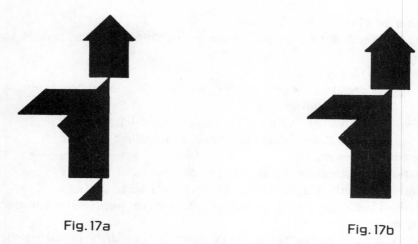

Fig. 17a   Fig. 17b

After you work on some of these tangram puzzles we provide, you will certainly want to create some of your own figures. We've shown you just a few:

— one letter, where you can build a whole alphabet;
— one number, where you can build all ten digits;
— one person, one boat, where you can create thousands of
  living and nonliving objects.

Other Tangram Sets

If you feel you've temporarily used up your creativity and imagination with these tangram pieces, Fig. 18 shows you another set you can build yourself, along with some of the figures you can make from them. You can also make tangram sets from the puzzles shown in Figs. 4, 5, 6 and 8 on pages 26 and 27.

Fig. 18

Games

Naturally you'll also want to use the tangrams in games you can play with your friends. We begin with a game in which you can use your new skills in copying outlines.

*TAN 1.
Aim of the Game: To copy a figure with tangram pieces when you are shown an outline.

Number of Players: Two or more.

Materials Needed: One set of tangram pieces for each player, pencils and paper.

How to Play: Each player

— Chooses four tangram pieces, and secretly constructs a figure,

— draws the outline of it,

— passes his/her outline to the player on the left,

— then builds the figure that matches the outline received.

First to do so wins.

Variation: Construct figures from 5 pieces, instead of 4.

Variation: Construct figures from all 7 pieces, instead of 4.

Variation: Each player does not tell how many pieces were used to construct the figure.

In this game, unlike the situation in mosaics, pieces can be joined together just at points and without corners touching.

When you attempt to build a figure that matches someone else's outline, use the same approach as we did in copying the boat:

— In your mind divide the figure into parts.

— Construct the approximate shape of one part.

— See what you need to add, change, or take away to make an exact copy of the original.

— Remember that certain parts, such as triangles and squares, can be made in many different ways. If one way uses up pieces you need for a different part of the figure, try another way.

Next we present a game in which you must use your knowledge of the sizes and shapes of the tangram pieces to cram them into a limited space.

*TAN 2.

Aim of the Game: To place the last tangram piece.

Number of Players: Two.

Materials Needed: A set of tangram pieces; a 3x3 grid.

How to Play: Players alternate turns. On each turn a player places one piece inside the border. It may touch but not overlap with another piece. It may not touch the border. Once placed a piece cannot be moved. The first player who cannot place a piece loses.

Variation: The piece placed may *not* touch another piece.

Fig. 19 shows a sample game.

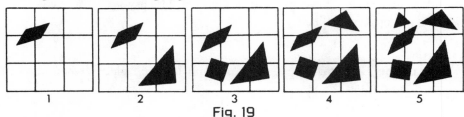

1   2   3   4   5

Fig. 19

On the third move Player A places the square in such a way that there will only be room for two more pieces. On the fourth move Player B places one. On the fifth move, Player A places the other, and wins.

Solutions

Page 31

4. 5 piece square

7 piece square: see Fig. 1

Pages 32 and 33

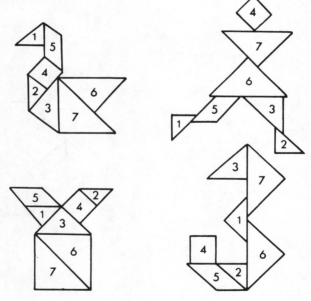

Page 34

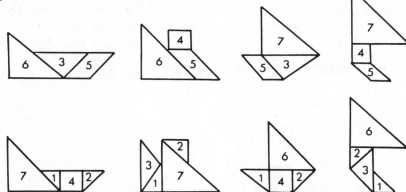

Page 35

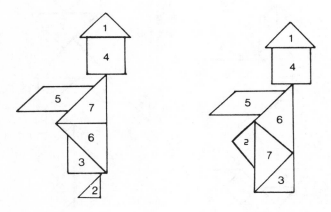

CHAPTER IV

MEET THE POLYNOMINOES!

A polynomino, like a mosaic, is a group of squares connected together at their edges so that their corners coincide. A polynomino differs from a mosaic, however, in two important ways:

— All the squares in a polynomino are the same color.

— The squares in a set of polynominoes are connected in all the possible ways to each other, not just arrangements that form rectangles.

In this chapter we explore what different polynominoes exist, and how we can put them together to form other shapes. We can apply what we learn from playing with polynominoes to problems of laying things out: arranging furniture in a room, arranging objects on a desk, packing a suitcase efficiently, storing food in a cupboard conveniently, etc.

We will begin by seeing how many different ways square tiles can be attached to each other to form polynominoes. We do not consider two shapes to be "different" if we can get from one to the other by rotation and/or by flipping over. For example, Fig. 1a becomes Fig. 1b by rotation, and becomes Fig. 1c by flipping over.

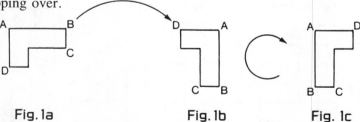

Fig. 1a Fig. 1b Fig. 1c

We refer to the polynominoes as follows:

—A single tile is a monomino [*mono* = one]
Each mosaic tile by itself is a monomino.

— Two tiles form a *domino* [*do* = two].

A domino can be put together in only one way. The arrangement in Fig. 2a is not different from that in Fig. 2b.

Fig. 2a   **Fig. 2b**

— Three tiles form a *tromino* [*tro* = three].

A tromino can be put together in two different ways, as a straight tromino or a right tromino, as in Fig. 3.

Fig. 3

— Four tiles form a *tetramino* [*tetra* = four].

A tetramino can be put together in five different ways.

These ways are given names and numbers in Fig. 4.

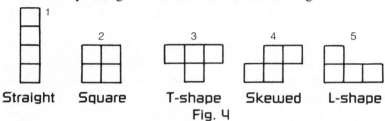

Straight   Square   T-shape   Skewed   L-shape

Fig. 4

— Five tiles form a *pentomino* [*pento* = five].

Fig. 5 shows the 12 different pentominoes. We give them the names of the letters they resemble so that we can refer to them and so that you can remember them.

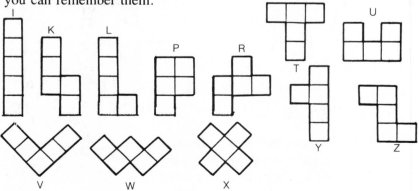

Fig. 5

Activities

Here are some activities to get you more familiar with different kinds of polynominoes and how they fit together.

Caution: Some activities may be impossible to carry out, but you can still learn from trying them . If you find yourself stuck on something, read further to see if you are working on one of the impossible tasks. Solutions for some of these activities appear only at the end of the chapter, so you have a chance to work on them on your own.

1.   Fill up completely each of the grids in Fig. 6 with dominoes according to the same rules:
— each domino covers exactly two grid boxes
— no domino overlaps another
— no domino extends beyond the grid.
Instead of using actual dominoes, draw them in where you think they go.

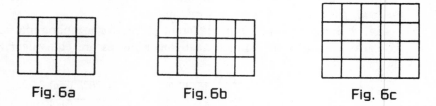

Fig. 6a   **Fig. 6b**   **Fig. 6c**

Fig. 6b cannot be filled up according to these conditions. Here's why. Each domino covers two boxes. An odd number can never be divided evenly by two. If a rectangle contains an odd total number of boxes (as a 3 x 5 rectangle contains 15 boxes), then you will never be able to fill it up completely with dominoes. There will always be one box left uncovered.

2.   Figure 7a contains 14 boxes, an even number. Fill it up with dominoes.

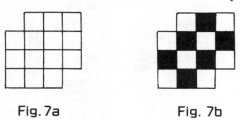

Fig. 7a   **Fig. 7b**

As you may suspect after trying a while, it is impossible to do this. Here's why.

Think of this figure marked up like a checkerboard, that is, with two colors alternating from box to box, as in Fig. 7b. You start with

8 white and 6 black boxes. Each domino you put down must cover one black and one white box. After you put down 6 dominoes, two white boxes will remain. Since a domino must cover one black and one white box, you can't cover the two leftover white boxes with one domino.

3.   Fill up a 4x4 grid using 5 straight trominoes and one monomino.

Fig. 8

Since a 4x4 grid has 16 boxes, 15 of them could be covered by 5 trominoes, and the 16th box by a monomino. Have you seen how?

Hint: You can only do it if you place the monomino in a corner of the grid, as in Fig 8. Let's see why this is so.

Fig. 9 shows the only three different places for a monomino on a 4x4 grid. Because of symmetry, all other places are equivalent, as shown by the dotted lines.

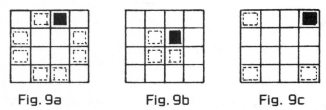

Fig. 9a   Fig. 9b   Fig. 9c

Suppose we place the monomino as in Fig. 9a. How then could the five tromino pieces be placed?

Look at the square marked "1" in Fig. 10a.

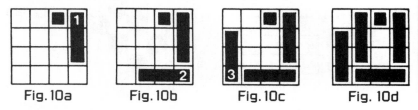

Fig. 10a   Fig. 10b   Fig. 10c   Fig. 10d

It can only be covered by the tromino shown.

— Then the square marked "2" can only be covered by the tromino in Fig. 10b.

— The square marked "3" can only be covered by the tromino shown in Fig. 10c.

— A fourth tromino can only be placed as shown in Fig. 10d.

This leaves three isolated squares that cannot be covered by a tromino.

Suppose we place the monomino as in Fig. 9b. How then could the five tromino pieces be placed?

Look at the square marked "1" in Fig. 11a.

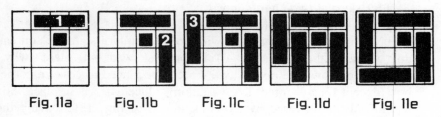

Fig. 11a   Fig. 11b   Fig. 11c   Fig. 11d   Fig. 11e

It might be covered by the tromino shown in Fig. 11a or the one shown in Fig. 12a. We'll look at both cases.

A.   If it is covered as in Fig. 11a,
   — Then the square marked "2" can only be covered by the tromino shown in Fig. 11b.
   — The square marked "3" can only be covered by the tromino in Fig. 11c.
   — A fourth tromino can be placed as shown either in Fig. 11d, Fig. 11e.

Either way three isolated squares are left that cannot be covered by a tromino.

B.   If it is covered by the tromino in Fig. 12a,

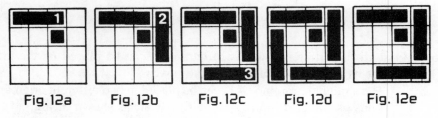

Fig. 12a   Fig. 12b   Fig. 12c   Fig. 12d   Fig. 12e

   — Then the square marked "2" can only be covered by the tromino shown in Fig. 12b.
   — The square marked "3" can only be covered by the tromino in Fig. 12c.
   — A fourth tromino can be placed as shown either in Fig. 12d, Fig. 12e.
   Either way three isolated squares are left that cannot be covered by a tromino.

4. Fill up a 4x4 grid using 5 *right* trominoes and one monomino. You can do this no matter where you place the monomino.

5. Fill up a 4 x 4 grid using only:
    — four straight (#1) tetraminoes
    — four square (#2) tetraminoes
    — four T-shaped (#3) tetraminoes
    — four skewed (#4) tetraminoes
    — four L-shaped (#5) tetraminoes

    Have you discovered not all will work to build a square? You can do it with all of them (Figs. 13a-d) except the skewed (#4). Here's why.

    Fig. 13e shows the only way a #5 can be placed to cover a corner box (except for a symmetrical variation). Once a #5 is in place, box X can only be covered by a #5 as shown in Fig. 13f, leaving the isolated box marked by ''Y.''

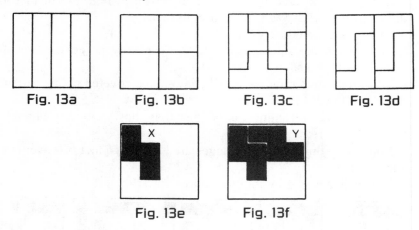

Fig. 13a   Fig. 13b   Fig. 13c   Fig. 13d

Fig. 13e   Fig. 13f

6. Find all the different ways each tetramino can be placed on the grid so that its corners coincide with grid boxes.
    — The straight tetramino (#1) can be placed in two different orientations on the grid, horizontal and vertical, as shown in Fig. 14.

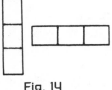

Fig. 14

    — The square tetramino (#2) can be placed in only one orientation on the grid, as shown in Fig. 15. It always looks the same.

Fig. 15

— The T-shape tetramino (#3) can be rotated into four different orientations on a grid, as in Fig. 16.

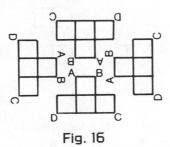

Fig. 16

— The skewed tetramino (#4) can only be rotated into two different positions on the grid. But since it is not symmetric, you can then flip it over, and get two more positions, as in Fig. 17.

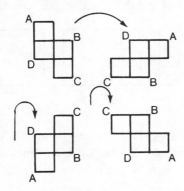

Fig. 17

— The L-shaped tetramino (#5) also is not symmetric. You can rotate it into four different positions, then flip it over, and by rotation get more positions, as in Fig. 18.

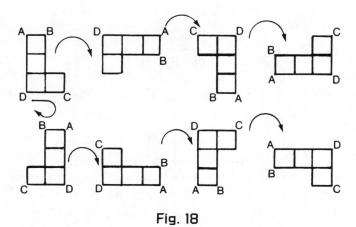

Fig. 18

7.   A pentomino and tetramino together contain nine squares. Find three
     ways to connect them to form a 3x3 grid.

8.   Two pentomino pieces together contain ten squares. Connect two pen-
     tomino pieces to form a 3x4 grid with two squares missing.
     — Do this in as many ways as you can.
     — After you get one, make a drawing of it to refer to later. Figure
        19 shows some of the different shapes you might have gotten.

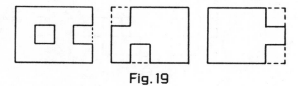

Fig. 19

Refer to your drawings. Did you get them all? Were there some you
got that we didn't show? Fifteen different ones are possible.
    You can produce two of these 15 in many different ways, as seen
in Fig. 20.

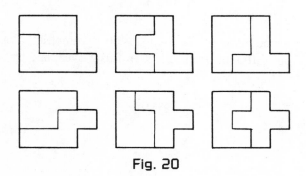

Fig. 20

Remember these combinations. Later we will do puzzles with pentomino pieces. If you see a gap shaped like that in Figure 20, you will be able to recall what combinations will fill it.

9. Three pentomino pieces together contain 15 squares. Connect them to form a 3x5 grid.
— Do it in five different ways.
   Here's a general approach to doing it:
— First create a 3 x 4 grid with two squares missing,
— Then add a piece to it.
This will not work with every 3 x 4 grid with two squares missing. Fig. 21 shows the ones it will work with:

Fig. 21

10. Put together 6 pentomino pieces to form a 5x6 grid.
   Do you see a general approach for doing this?
— Make two 3x5 grids from different pieces,
— Then put them together (Fig. 22).

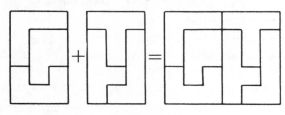

Fig. 22

Work on Your Own

1. Place all the 12 pentomino pieces into an 8x8 grid.
   — An 8x8 grid contains 64 squares. Since 12 pentominoes cover just 60 squares ($12 \times 5 = 60$), four uncovered squares will remain somewhere on the grid.
2. Now do the same thing, with the empty squares at the corners.
3. Do the same thing with the empty squares all moved
   (a) one,
   (b) two, and
   (c) three squares diagonally toward the center.
      Fig. 23 shows the solution for 3(a).

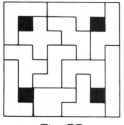

Fig. 23

4.   Place all the pieces into a 4x15 grid with *no* empty squares.

Now that you are familiar with the polynomino pieces, here are some games you can play with them. In the first game, players alternate placing tromino pieces inside a limited space. The last player to place a piece wins.

Games

*POLY 1.

Aim of the Game: To place the last tromino piece on a 5x5 grid.

Number of Players: Two or more.

Materials Needed: 4 straight and 4 right tromino pieces, 5x5 grid.

How to Play: Each player in turn places any tromino piece so that
— it exactly covers 3 grid squares, and
— it doesn't overlap with a piece already there.

A piece once placed on the grid cannot be moved. A player who is unable to place a piece loses.

Fig. 24 shows an example of a game played by two players.

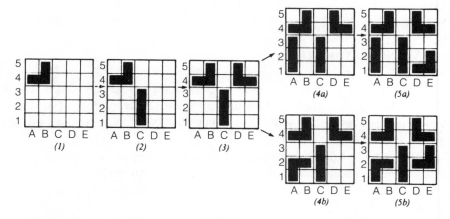

Fig. 24

Player A makes move 1.
- Of the 25 squares at the start, 22 are still empty. But one of them, at A5, cannot be used to place a tromino. So 21 squares are still available and a maximum of 7 (21/3 = 7) trominoes can still be placed.

Player B makes move 2.
- Now 18 squares are still available, and a maximum of 6 trominoes can still be placed.

Player A makes move 3.
- Three more squares (at C4, C5 and E5) have been blocked off, leaving 12 squares still available. A maximum of 4 trominoes can still be placed.

If Player B makes move 4a...
- 9 squares will still be available. Player A can win by making move 5a. There will be six squares then available, with room for exactly two more trominoes, Player B's, then Player A's.
If Player B makes move 4b...
- 3 more squares will have been blocked off (at A3, B1 and B3), and 6 will still be available. Player A can win by making move 5b. This will block off 3 more squares (at D1, D3 and E1), and there will be no squares available.

Variation: Use 7x7 grid, instead of 5x5.

*POLY 2.
Aim of the Game: To place the last tetramino piece on a 8x8 grid.
Number of Players: Two or more.
Materials Needed: 8x8 grid; pencil.
How to Play: Each player in turn draws any tetramino piece on the grid so that
- it exactly covers 4 grid squares, and
- it doesn't overlap with a piece already there.

A piece once drawn on the grid cannot be moved. A player who is unable to place a piece loses.

Variation 1: Use the set of 12 pentominoes instead of straight tetraminoes; each player can place any pentomino on each turn; 8x8 grid.
Variation 2: Players agree beforehand on what kinds of polynominoes will be used and on the size of the grid.

Fig. 25 shows the final position of a game played by two players.

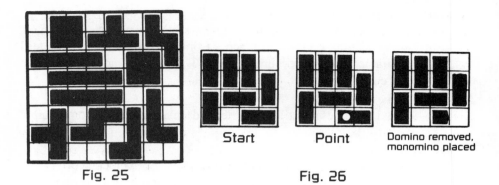

Start   Point   Domino removed, monomino placed

Fig. 25   Fig. 26

In the next game, one player tries to drive the other player's domino pieces off the grid.

*POLY 3.

Aim of the Game: For Player A, to rid the grid of domino pieces as quickly as possible. For Player B, to force Player A to use as many monominoes as possible.

Number of Players: Two.

Materials Needed: Set of 7 dominoes; 12 monominoes, 4x4 grid.

How to Play:

a. Player B places all seven domino pieces on the grid, so that each covers 2 grid squares exactly and doesn't overlap with another piece.

b. Player A chooses and points to one grid square covered by a domino.

c. Player B must then either
    — move that domino to another location on the grid (without overlapping another piece and without using the square that was pointed to or
    — remove the domino piece.

d. Player A then puts a monomino on the square pointed to.

The game continues with Player A pointing to squares and Player B moving dominoes until all the dominoes have been removed.

The monominoes on the grid are counted. Player B gets one point for each monomino used. Then Players A and B switch roles. The player with the most points wins.

Variation 1: Player A uses 12 monominoes, Player B uses any 5 trominoes.

Fig. 26 shows the beginning moves in a game of POLY 3.

*POLY 4.

Aim of the Game: For Player A, to rid the grid of tetramino pieces as quickly as possible. For Player B, to force Player A to use as many monominoes as possible.

Number of Players: Two.

Materials Needed: Set of tetramino pieces (one of each shape); 10 monominoes; 4x4 grid.

How to Play:

a.   Player B places all five tetramino pieces on the grid, so that each covers 4 grid squares exactly and doesn't overlap with another piece.

b.   Player A chooses and points to one grid square covered by a tetramino.

c.   Player B must then either

— move that tetramino to another location on the grid (without overlapping another piece and without using the square that was pointed to, or

— remove the tetramino piece.

d.   Player A then puts a monomino on the square pointed to.

The game continues with Player A pointing to squares and Player B moving tetraminoes until all the tetraminoes have been removed.

The monominoes on the grid are counted. Player B gets on point for each monomino used. Then Players A and B switch roles. The player with the most points wins.

Variation 1: On a 8x8 grid, Player A uses as many monominoes as needed, Player B uses a set of pentominoes.

Fig. 27 shows a sample game of POLY 4.

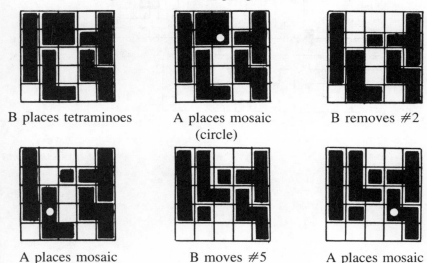

B places tetraminoes   A places mosaic   B removes #2
                                  (circle)

A places mosaic   B moves #5   A places mosaic

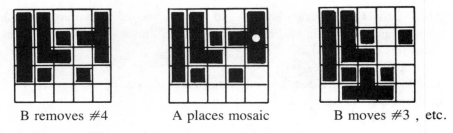

B removes #4   A places mosaic   B moves #3 , etc.

Fig. 27

SOLUTIONS

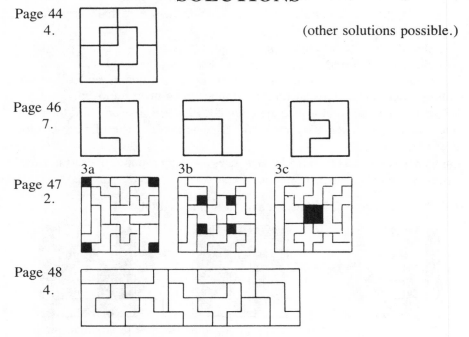

Page 44
4.

(other solutions possible.)

Page 46
7.

Page 47
2.

3a   3b   3c

Page 48
4.

CHAPTER V

FILLING SPACE

In the Mosaics chapter, we put together square tiles to form designs and pictures. In each of the Puzzles, Tangram and Polynominoes chapters, we put together a set of shapes *different* from each other to form other designs and pictures. Now in this chapter, we repeat the *same* shape to fill up a space. We call this *tesselation.*"

In the introductory chapter you saw one simple tesselation problem: how to fill up the area of a parallelogram with triangles. This type of problem has direct applications to practical situations where you want to put many same-size objects in the smallest possible space:

— cutting out identical pieces from a large piece of material with minimal waste
— saving fabric when making clothing.
— saving sheet metal in industrial applications.
— planning the layout of a new parking lot.
— placing merchandise efficiently on a store shelf.
— placing boxes or cans of food on a home cupboard shelf.

Tesselation also has a less direct application to other situations where you want to pack objects of *different* size into the smallest possible space:

— packing a suitcase
— packing suitcases into the trunk of your car
— arranging furniture in an apartment or house.

First we will explain some terms used with tesselation, then show you some simple figures that tesselate, give you practice in tesselating other figures we present, in creating your own tesselations, and an opportunity to apply the ideas of tesselation in some practical situations.

Some Definitions

Fig. 1 shows a way to classify simple figures that is useful to us in tesselation.

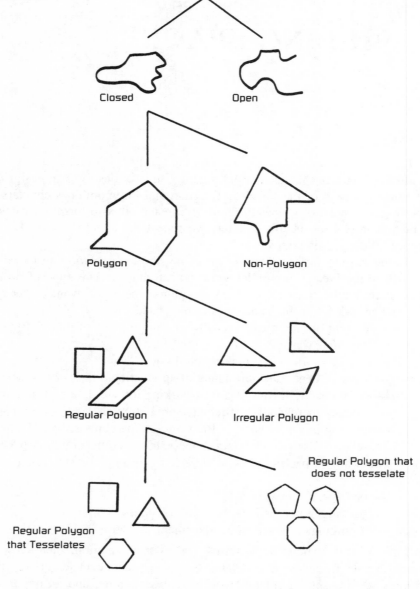

— A *closed figure* is one you can trace completely starting from any point.
— An *open figure* has a gap that doesn't allow you to do this.
— A closed figure made up only of straight lines is called a *polygon*.

— A closed figure with one or more curved lines is *not* a polygon.
— A polygon with all sides equal in length is called a *regular* polygon. A "square" is simply the special name for a regular polygon with four sides.

Tesselation means repeating the same figure many times to fill up an area that extends indefinitely
— with no gaps between figures, and
— without the figures overlapping.

Fig. 2a shows that a square tesselates: it can repeat, without gaps or overlap, to fill an area that extends indefinitely.

A figure that tesselates may or may not be able to fill up an area with definite limits.

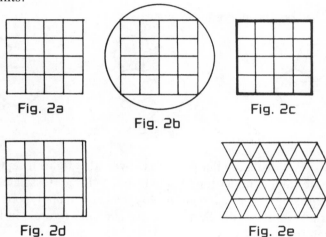

Fig. 2a   **Fig. 2b**   **Fig. 2c**

Fig. 2d   **Fig. 2e**

— Fig. 2b shows that a square cannot fill up a circular area without gaps.
— A square may (Fig. 2c) or may not (Fig. 2d) fill up a rectangular area without gaps, depending on the sizes of the square and of the rectangular area.
— A triangle can fill up an area that extends indefinitely (Fig. 2c), but may or may not fill up a rectangular area.

What Figures Tesselate?

Some closed figures tesselate, and others do not.
Just three kinds of regular polygons tesselate:
1. triangles △
2. squares □
3. hexagons ⬡

Fig. 3 shows how each tesselates.

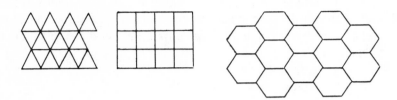

Fig. 3

No other regular polygon tesselates.

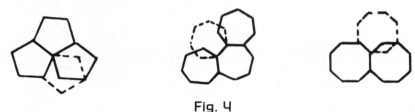

Fig. 4

Fig. 4 shows that a regular pentagon (five-sided figure), septagon (seven-sided figure) and octagon (eight-sided figure) do not tesselate.

But surprisingly, many *irregular* polygons and nonpolygons (shapes with curved lines) do tesselate. Some of these irregular figures, in fact, give the most interesting results.

You can tesselate *any* triangle and any four-sided polygon, whether regular or not. Here's how:

In Fig. 5a, we begin with an irregular triangle (the sides are not all equal). The points of the triangle are labelled A, B and C.

Fig. 5a   **Fig. 5b**

Cut out a cardboard the size and shape of the triangle, and label its corners A, B and C. Use the cardboard to trace the triangle on a sheet of paper, and label the corners on the paper.

Rotate the cardboard so that A on the cardboard touches B on the paper, and B on the cardboard touches A on the paper (Fig. 5b). Trace the new triangle.

Now rotate the cardboard so that C on the cardboard touches A on the original triangle, and A on the cardboard touches C on the original triangle (Fig. 5c). Trace the new triangle.

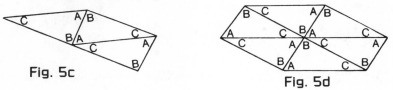

Fig. 5c

Fig. 5d

Continue rotating the cardboard so that sides are reversed (AB - BA; BC - CB; and AC - CA) around a central point, and tracing the new triangles, as in Fig. 5d.

You can use the same method to tesselate any regular or irregular four-sided polygon (Fig. 6).

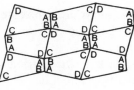

Fig. 6

Two figures, each of which tesselates by itself, may also tesselate together, as do the hexagon and four-sided figure in Fig. 7a. Even a figure that does *not* tesselate by itself, like the regular pentagon (five-sided figure), may tesselate when combined with another figure, as in Fig. 7b.

Fig. 7a

Fig. 7b

Activities

1. Show how to tesselate the triangle in Fig. 8.
2. Show how to tesselate the four-sided figure in Fig. 9.

Fig. 8   Fig. 9

3.   Tesselate each of the tetraminoes (See last chapter if you don't remember what they are).
4.   Find out which of the pentominoes can tesselate by themselves, and which can tesselate in combination with others.

Creating Your Own Tesselations

Let's see how you can create your own tesselations. Start with a figure that tesselates, and move a segment of it from one place to another, keeping the *area* of the figure the same.

Fig. 10a shows how you take a symmetrical chunk away from one side of a square and put it on the opposite side.

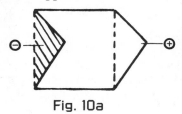

Fig. 10a

You can also
— take away an assymetrical chunk (Fig. 10b),

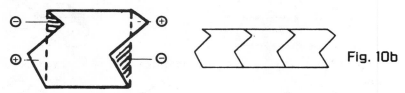

Fig. 10b

— take away a curved chunk (Fig. 10c),

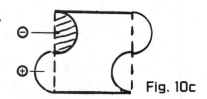

Fig. 10c

— take away a chunk from half of one side, place it on the other half; then do the same with an adjacent side (Fig. 10d).

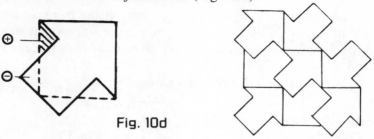

Fig. 10d

— divide a hexagon into six large triangles (Fig. 11a); subdivide each into 16 smaller triangles to use as a guide (Fig. 11b); then take away a chunk from one side of a large triangle, place it on another side of that same triangle (Fig. 11c), then do the same with the other large triangles (Fig. 11d).

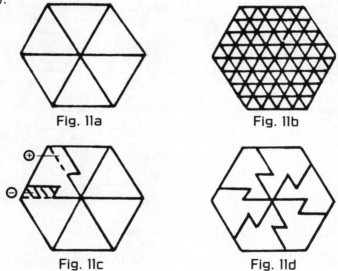

Fig. 11a   **Fig. 11b**

Fig. 11c   **Fig. 11d**

Fig. 12 shows some other tesselations you could get in this same general way.

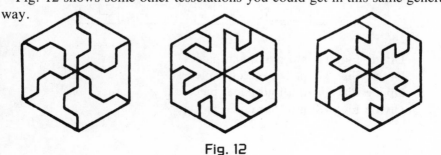

Fig. 12

Dividing Spaces

You have been learning how to create new shapes that tesselate and can be used to fill up a space. Now let's reverse the process; beginning with a fixed space, how can we divide it into a given number of pieces of the same size and shape?

1.   Divide a square into two equal parts.

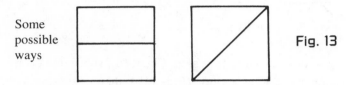

Some possible ways   Fig. 13

2.   Divide a square into two equal parts in some other ways. Hint: The methods you have just used in dividing a hexagon can be used here too. Divide the square first as shown by dotted lines in Fig. 14. Then Fig. 14 shows some possibilities for dividing it further.

Fig. 14

3.   Divide the square in Fig. 15 into two equal parts.

Fig. 15

4.   Divide the square in Fig. 16 into four equal parts.

— Divide it into two equal parts, then subdivide each part.

Fig. 16

5.   Divide Fig. 17 into two equal pieces.
6.   Divide Fig. 17 into three equal pieces.
7.   Divide Fig. 17 into four equal pieces.
8.   Divide Fig. 18 into four equal pieces.

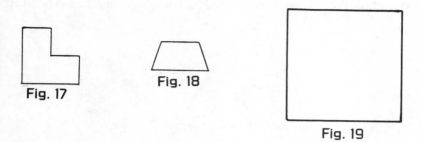

Fig. 17

Fig. 18

Fig. 19

9. Divide Fig. 19 into five equal pieces.
10. Use four straight lines to divide Fig. 20 into six squares.

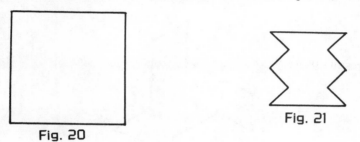

Fig. 20

Fig. 21

11. Use three straight lines to divide Fig. 21 into six triangles.

More Activities

Find your own other ways to make more complicated tesselations. You can add interest by decorating the tesselation figure you create (Fig. 22).

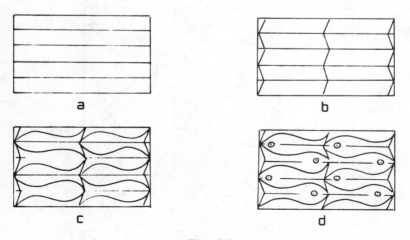

a

b

c

d

Fig. 22

1. Show how Fig. 23 can be developed from a square, and then tesselate it.

Fig. 23

2. Show how Fig. 24 can be developed from a triangle, and then tesselate it.

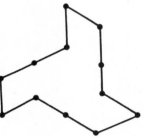

Fig. 24

3. Sometimes a design seems to be made up of complicated elements but really is made up of simple elements (as in Figs. 33-36 in the Mosaics chapter). Fig. 25 shows another example of a complicated design. Can you find the single element that allows you to construct this design by tesselation? (Hint: it is a six-sided figure.)

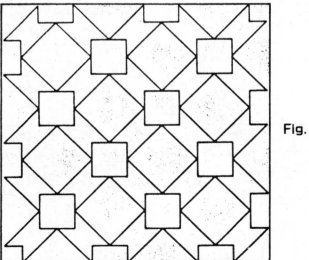

Fig. 25

4. Some shapes can both tesselate and be used to build larger scale models of themselves. For example, a square tesselates, and four together as in Fig. 26 will form a bigger square. Show how the shape in Fig. 27 tesselates and can be used to form a larger scale version of itself.

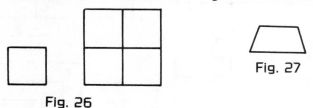

Fig. 27

Fig. 26

Solutions

P. 58   1.

2.

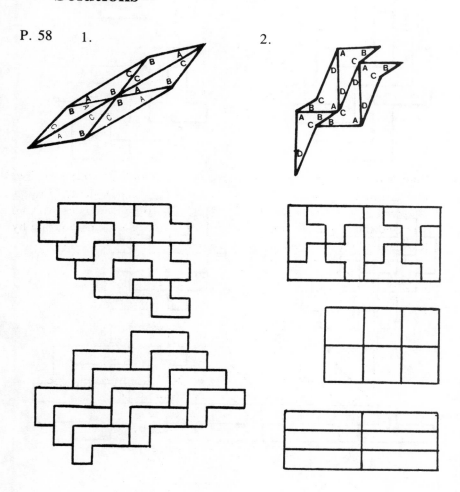

4.

Page 61

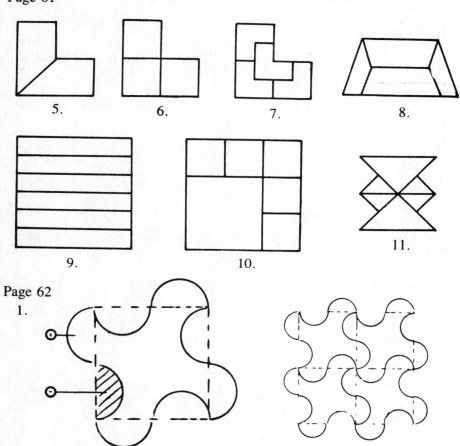

5.   6.   7.   8.

9.   10.   11.

Page 62
1.

2.

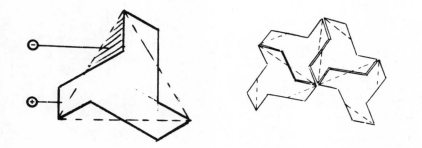

Page 63

4.

CHAPTER VI

MAZES

You probably already are familiar with some mazes, in which you must avoid blind alleys and find a path from point A to point B. In this chapter you will learn about several different kinds of mazes: what they are, how to build them, how to solve them, how to play games with them, and how to apply what you've learned about mazes to solve practical problems.

The "MANY-TO-MANY" Maze

Let's begin with a "many-to-many" maze as shown in Fig. 1.

Fig. 1

There are four separate lines that go from top to bottom. The lines obey these rules:
- Only two lines cross at the same point.
- Lines cross each other at approximately 90 degree angles.
- A line continues in the same direction after crossing another line.
  Where do the lines that start at #1, #2, #3 and #5 end?
  You can go through a maze in two ways:
- by moving an object like a pencil or toothpick as a pointer along the path (holding the pencil just a little bit off the paper, not to draw lines), or
- by tracing a path in your mind only.
    Each way you use somewhat different abilities. When you use a pointer, you always know what point you're up to. When you trace a path in your

mind only, you may get confused about what point you're up to.

Guiding your eye through the maze with a pointer, then, doesn't require as much skill as going through in your mind. Therefore, first do each maze activity we suggest with a pointer. When you have increased your skill and feel confident, do the same activity tracing your path by eye only.

Fig. 2 gives you another two many-to-many mazes. Do them, and check with the answers at the end of the chapter.

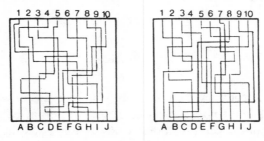

Fig. 2

Making your Own Many-to-Many Maze

You can create your own many-to-many maze, and, even though you have created it yourself, still enjoy and benefit from solving it. Here's how:

a.   Box off an 11 x 11 piece of graph paper (Fig. 3a).

b.   Mark ten points at the top and ten at the bottom (Fig. 3a).

c.   Connect each top point to a bottom point not directly below it (Fig. 3b). After you make your first connection, keep in mind these three rules:
   ● Only two lines cross at the same point.
   ● Lines cross each other at approximately 90 degree angles.
   ● A line continues in the same direction after crossing another line.

d.   Label the top ten points from 1-10 across, and the bottom ten points from A-J (Fig. 3c). By putting in the labels only at the end, you prevent yourself from learning what number goes with what letter, so you can trace the paths as if someone else had created the maze.

You are ready now to trace each numbered line in turn from top to bottom.

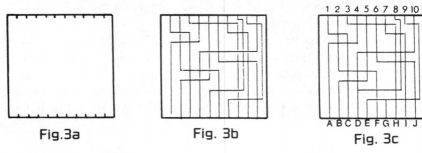

Fig.3a   Fig. 3b

Fig. 3c

You can also make your own mazes "free-hand" with curved lines, and without using graph paper, as in Fig. 4.

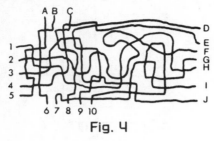

Fig. 4

A Maze Game

*MAZES 1.
Aim of the Game: To be the first to complete a many-to-many maze.
Number of Players: Two.
Materials Needed: Graph paper; pencils.
How to Play: Each player draws a ten-line many-to-many maze on a graph paper grid, according to the following rules:

— Only two lines cross at the same point.
— Lines cross each other at approximately 90 degree angles.
— A line continues in the same direction after crossing another line.

The beginning points of the lines are labelled from 1 to 10, and the end points from A to J.

The players exchange mazes and attempt to solve each other's maze. The first player to trace all ten lines says so. If they have all been correctly traced, that player wins. If not, each player gets one point for each line correctly traced, and loses three points for each line incorrectly traced. The player with more points wins.

Variation: Each player draws ten lines free-hand, instead of on a graph paper grid.

Line and Path Mazes

The Line Maze

Let's turn next to a simple kind of maze called the *line maze* (Fig. 5). In this kind of maze, you move along a line toward a goal, changing direction if you wish when the line meets another line. This is different from the many-to-many maze, in which you *cannot* change direction where two lines meet.

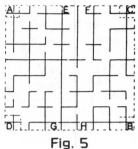

Fig. 5

The Path Maze

In the *path maze* (Fig. 6a), instead of moving along a line, you move *between* two lines, never touching or crossing them, as you try to reach a goal. There are many "living" path mazes in which the "lines" are garden hedges or bushes.

In Fig. 6a your first choice point is at "A."
— If you go left, you exit from the maze at the top.
— If you go down, you can reach the opposite corner as shown.
— If you go right, you can reach the opposite corner as shown in Fig. 6b.

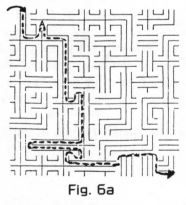

Fig. 6a

Fig. 6b

A Real Path Maze

Some day you may find yourself inside a real path maze such as one formed by garden hedges, or a paper one, where your goal is to get out. Here's a rule that may be helpful: Stick to one side of the path as you travel. This will always lead you eventually to the outside (Fig. 7) unless the maze contains an "island" (Fig. 8).

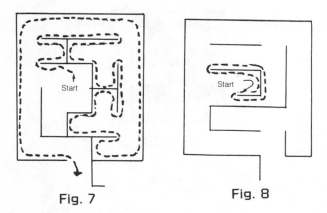

Fig. 7   Fig. 8

If you follow this rule and the maze does contain an island, you will merely circle that island. By marking your path choices (as with a piece of chalk), you can then avoid making the same choice twice.

The Rule Maze

A rule maze has rules that tell you which paths you can and cannot take. Usually the rule maze is made up of boxes, and you move from one box to another with a common border.

Suppose, for example, the maze were made up of three different kinds of elements, A, B and C. The rules could state that you can go only from A to B, from B to C, and from C to A. This means you can never go from A to A, from A to C, from B to A, from B to B, from C to B, and from C to C.

Fig. 9a shows a path you could take from one corner to the opposite corner of a maze with just that rule.

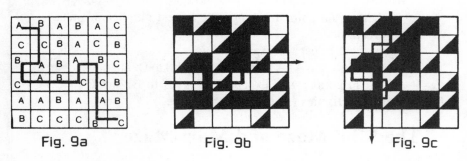

Fig. 9a   Fig. 9b   Fig. 9c

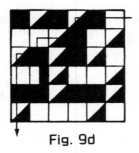

Fig. 9d

Activities with the Rule Maze

Mix up 12 each of your black, white, and diagonally half- black, half-white mosaic tile pieces to form a 6x6 rule maze, where
— "A" is a black tile,
— "B" is a half black/half white tile, and
— "C" is a white tile.
Try each of the following activities, with the rules given above.
1.   Find a path from anywhere on the left side of the maze to anywhere on the right side (Fig. 9b).
2.   Find a path from anywhere on the top side of the maze to anywhere on the bottom side (Fig. 9c).
3.   Find a path from the upper left hand tile to the lower right hand tile.
4.   Find a path from the upper right hand tile to the lower left tile (Fig. 9d).
5.   Mix your tiles together again, and repeat (1) through (4) with a new arrangement of the tiles.
     In each case,
     — if you found a path, see if it is the shortest possible path (the one that goes through the fewest tiles).
     If it isn't, find the shortest path now.
     — If there is no path, rearrange the fewest number of pieces to create one.
     Change the rules, for example,
     — you can go A to A, A to B, B to A, and B to B, but never enter a C.
     — You can go any way except A to A, B to B, and C to C.
Then repeat the activities (1) through (5) above.

The Mini-Maze and Maxi-Maze

In both the mini-maze and the maxi-maze, you go from starting box to finish box. Each box has a certain number value. When you enter a box, you add its value to your total score. The same maze can serve as a "mini-

maze'' and as a ''maxi-maze,'' but the goals and rules will be different in each case. The goal for the mini-maze:
— accumulate the *lowest* point total possible.
The goal for the maxi-maze:
— accumulate the highest point total possible, as you enter a fixed number of boxes.

In both the mini-maze and the maxi-maze you move from box to box horizontally or vertically, but not diagonally.

Let's look at some examples.

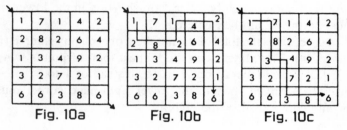

Fig. 10a   Fig. 10b   Fig. 10c

Think of Fig. 10a as a *mini-maze*. The path shown in Fig. 10b gives you the lowest possible score (28 points).

Now think of Fig. 10a as a *maxi-maze* where you may enter only 8 boxes in going from start to finish. The path shown in Fig. 10c gives you the highest total points possible (56).

Here are some games to play with mini-mazes and maxi-mazes.

*MAZES 2.
Aim of the Game: To get from one corner to the opposite corner with the lowest point total.
Number of Players: Two or more.
Materials Needed: 5x5 grid on graph paper.
Preparation: Fill the grid by repeating the numbers 1, 2, 3, 4 and 5 in a mixed-up order. Make exact copies of the grid for each player.
How to Play: Each player starts in the upper left-hand box of his/her own grid, and traces a path with a pencil, moving from box to box up, down, left or right (but not diagonally) until the ''finish'' box in the lower right-hand corner is reached. Each player receives the total of the numbers of each box entered (including the first and last). The player with the lowest total of points wins. It does not matter how many boxes a player has entered.
Variation: Use the numbers from 1 to 10, instead of 1 to 5.

Here now is a maxi-maze game:

*MAZES 3.

Aim of the Game: To get from one corner to the opposite corner, entering exactly eight boxes, with the highest point total.

Number of Players: Two or more.

Materials Needed: 5x5 grid on graph paper.

Preparation: Fill the grid by repeating the numbers 1, 2, 3, 4 and 5 in a mixed-up order. Make exact copies of the grid for each player.

How to Play: Each player starts in the upper left-hand box of his/her own grid, and traces a path with a pencil, moving from box to box up, down, left or right (but not diagonally). The "finish" box in the lower right-hand corner must be the eighth box entered.

Each player receives the total of the numbers of each box entered (including the first and last). The player with the highest total of points wins.

Variation: Use the numbers from 1 to 10, instead of 1 to 5.

Variation: The "finish" box in the lower right-hand corner must be the *tenth* box entered, instead of the eighth.

Applying Maze-Ability

Make heavy dots on graph paper to carry out the following five activities.

1. Here are nine dots. Draw four straight lines, without taking your pencil off the paper, that go through all the dots.

    . . .

    . . .

    . . .

2. Here are 16 dots. Draw six straight lines, without taking your pencil off the paper, that go through all the dots.

    . . . .

    . . . .

    . . . .

    . . . .

3. Here are 64 dots. Draw 15 straight lines, without taking your pencil off the paper, that start at dot A, go through all the dots, and end at dot B. The lines may not cross each other.

4.   Here are 64 dots. Draw straight lines, without taking your pencil off
the paper, that start at dot A, go through all the dots, and end at dot
B. The lines may not cross each other.
a.   Use as many lines as possible.
b.   Use as few lines as possible.

5.   Here are 64 dots. Draw straight lines, without taking your pencil off
the paper, that start at dot A, go through all the dots, and end at dot
B. The lines may not cross each other.
a.   Use as many lines as possible.
b.   Use as few lines as possible.

Solutions

Page 68

Left	1. I	6. A	Right	1. F	6. H
	2. G	7. D		2. A	7. I
	3. E	8. F		3. J	8. C
	4. B	9. J		4. D	9. E
	5. C	10. H		5. G	10. B

Page 74

1.   2.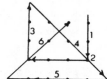

3.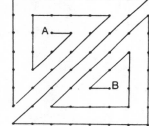

Page 75

4.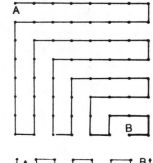

5a. 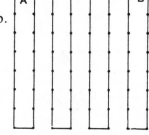   5b.

CHAPTER VII

Observation

In this chapter we deal with your ability to observe. This includes finding an object, comparing an object with others, estimating numbers of objects, and estimating areas. All of these activities are, as we shall see, important in everyday life.

Finding An Object

Comparing an Object with Others

A basic visual skill is to judge whether two objects are the same or different. If the objects are complicated, this might not be so easy. For example, are Figs. 1a and 1b the same or different?

Fig. 1a   Fig. 1b

When two objects are very similar, it's good to have a systematic way to compare them. One effective strategy is to break each object up in your mind into smaller units, and then compare these smaller units. For example,
— You might first divide a 6x6 square in your mind into four 3x3 squares. Then you would systematically compare upper left squares, then upper

right squares, then lower left squares, and finally lower right squares (Fig. 2).

— In comparing pictures, for example, you might compare two faces feature by feature; the two noses, then the two mouths, etc.

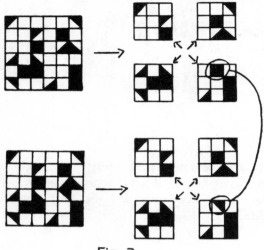

Fig. 2

We will now present a game so you can increase your skill in observing by comparing objects.

*OBS 1.

Aim of the Game: To quickly find out if two objects are identical or different.

Number of Players: Two.

Materials Needed: Mosaic pieces.

How to Play: Player A

— secretly sets up two identical 6x6 grids of mosaic pieces.

— may (or may not) change one or more of the mosaic pieces.

— shows the two grids to Player B.

Player B must state that the two grids are identical, or show each place they are different. A player who falsely says the two grids are identical when they are not or who says they are different when they are identical automatically loses.

Player A keeps track of the time Player B requires. Then players switch roles. Player who takes less time wins.

Variation: Use the line sides of the mosaic pieces.

Finding the Hidden Line Drawing

Another basic visual ability is to notice an object. We usually take this for granted, but sometimes an object may be hard to spot. For example, can you find the figure from Fig. 3 in exactly the same orientation, hidden in Fig. 4?

Let's see how you could find it.

— One way is to break down Fig. 3 into two more familiar parts, as a square and a triangle, as in Fig. 5. Then you could look for each part separately in Fig. 4.

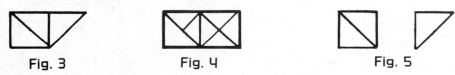

Fig. 3   **Fig. 4**   **Fig. 5**

Let's look for the square first. Fig. 4 has two squares:

— we can disregard the one on the right, because there is no place for the triangle.

— But the one on the left is promising: we can find the triangle to complete the target figure.

— You could also break down Fig. 3 into two triangles,

and look for them in Fig. 4. Fig. 4 has two of △

— We can disregard the one on the right, because there is no place for the ▽. But the one on the left yields:

— Instead of breaking down Fig. 3 into familiar complete figures (a square and a triangle) we could also look for fragments such as the ⌐ or the >.

When you find a fragment, follow its lines to see if it continues the way the model does.

Here are some models and larger figures in which they are hidden. Find them.

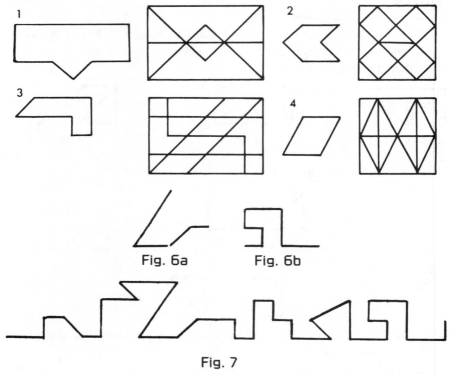

Fig. 6a   Fig. 6b

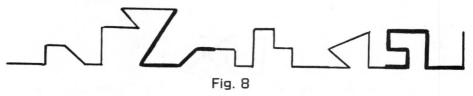

Fig. 7

Part of a line may also be hidden within a line, for example, Fig. 6a and 6b are contained in Fig. 7, as you can see in Fig. 8.

Fig. 8

Here are two more examples of part of a line hidden within a line. Find them.

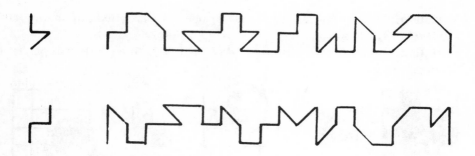

Finding the Hidden Mosaic Drawing

Now we give you some other models which you must find hidden in *mosaic* drawings, instead of line drawings. These models consist of solid black blobs. Again you should try to break up the model into smaller pieces of features. For example, if the model is ➤ , you might break it up in your mind into this ◢▮➤ and look for each piece separately.

Figs. 9a and 9b show some models and larger figures in which they are hidden. Find them.

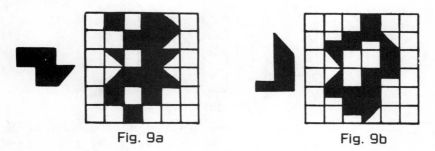

Fig. 9a   Fig. 9b

A Finding Game with Mosaic Drawings

Let's use the pieces in some games and activities to improve your ability to find hidden objects.

*OBS 2.

Aim of the Game: To find the hidden figure as quickly as possible.

Number of Players: Two.

Materials Needed: Mosaic pieces.

How to Play: Player A sets up a 4x4 square of mosaic pieces (Fig. 10) and separately, from two to four mosaic pieces sharing common sides (Fig. 11). Player B must show in what place or places these pieces occur in the same orientation in the square (Fig. 12). Player A keeps track of the time required. Then players switch roles. Player who takes less time wins.

Variation: The two pieces may touch at one corner, instead of sharing a side (Fig. 13).

Variation: Use 6x6 grid, instead of 4x4, and two, three or four separate touching pieces.

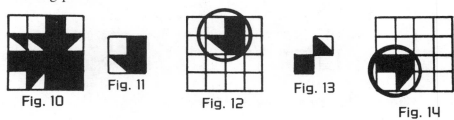

Fig. 10   Fig. 11   Fig. 12   Fig. 13   Fig. 14

Note that the circled pieces in Fig. 14 are *not* in the same orientation as the four pieces Player A has chosen for Player B to find.

Find the Word

Words too can be difficult to find. Can you find and read the word in Fig. 15?

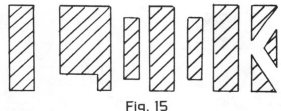

Fig. 15

If in your mind you draw imaginary lines along the top and along the bottom of the drawing, you may see the word more easily. It is given at the end of the chapter.

Finding Objects With Common Characteristics

Earlier in this chapter you practiced:
1. comparing two objects to see if they are identical (Is an object the same as a model?)
2. finding a hidden object the same as a model, and
3. finding two identical objects without a model.

Now you will combine all these skills, to find hidden objects that share the same characteristic but are not identical.

For example, Figs. 19a, b, c and d all show the same characteristic (they are triangles), but they are not identical. They differ in their sizes and angles.

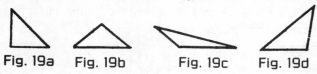

Fig. 19a   **Fig. 19b**   **Fig. 19c**   **Fig. 19d**

Fig. 20 (left) contains six triangles! Can you find them all? Here they are:

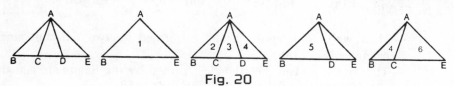

Fig. 20

1.   ABE
2.   ABC
3.   ACD

4.   ADE
5.   ABD
6.   ACE

Some may be "hidden," but all share the same characteristic of being triangles.

1.   Count the number of triangles in Figs. 15a, 15b, and 15c.

Fig. 15a

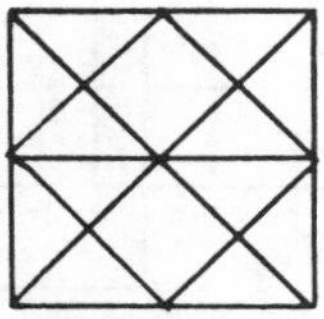

Fig. 15b

Fig. 15c

2.   Count the number of squares in Fig. 15b and Fig. 16.

Fig. 16

3.   Count the number of rectangles in Fig. 16.

Fig. 17

Do you have a systematic way of counting these objects? Let's look together at the number of *triangles* in Fig. 17.

— First we'll go clockwise around the figure, numbering the smallest triangles, as in Fig. 18a.

Fig. 18a   **Fig. 18b**   **Fig. 18c**   **Fig. 18d**

— Next we'll look at the triangles formed by two adjacent small triangles (Fig. 18b).
— Then we'll add in the triangles formed by the diagonals and the outside borders of the figures (Fig. 18c, 18d).

So we see this relatively simple figure contains 16 triangles.

4.   Now count the number of rectangles in Fig. 19.

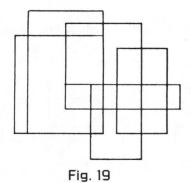

Fig. 19

Finding Letters

A printed page gives you an opportunity to apply the observation skills you have been practicing.

— The "same" letter of the alphabet appears in print in different ways. For example, the letter "e" appears as "E," "e," and as an italicized "*e*," but all share the common characteristic of being e's.
— A letter is also hidden when it is in a word.

Read the following sentence:

        FINISHED FILES ARE THE RE-
        SULT OF YEARS OF SCIENTIF-
        IC STUDY COMBINED WITH THE
        EXPERIENCE OF MANY YEARS.

Read it again, counting the number of times the letter ''f'' appears in any form. Most people do not notice all six; did you?

Activities

Count the number of times that each of the following letter(s) appears in the paragraph framed below:
1. an ''e.''
2. a ''t.''
3. an ''a.''
4. a ''u.''
5. an ''ea'' in any form as consecutive letters.
6. an ''in'' in any form as consecutive letters.
7. an ''ed'' in any form as consecutive letters.
8. a ''ter'' in any form as consecutive letters.

Each player draws at least twenty dots inside the same square. Each player then has five seconds to look at the square, and guess the total number of dots inside it. The guesses are written down. The dots are then counted, and the player who is closest (above or below the actual total) wins.

Finding Numbers

```
51238  54213288  54696  32581475  89243  12722651
10241  50371965  17321  23712137  13216  54541313
21213  25487813  13135  32652116  13116  45413794
79445  31356451  64845  66146826  91316  61464665
46516  55451644  44484  31312431  39314  44646444
87813  13135326  52116  13301570  50464  67312986
12181  37841649  84684  34157313  65561  98133117
47589  94375943  75902  84969571  94375  98543875
```

---

1. 3
2. 5
3. 8

4.   26 as consecutive numbers
5.   75 as consecutive numbers
6.   34 as consecutive numbers
7.   823 as consecutive numbers
8.   256 as consecutive numbers
9.   919 as consecutive numbers

On your own, take a page from a telephone book, and count as in activities (1) to (9) above. Compare your results with those of a friend.

Estimating

In the previous section you counted the number of objects you saw. In some situations where it is not possible to count, you must make estimates of what you see.

The Number of Objects You See

For example, look at Fig. 20 for five seconds, and estimate how many dots are inside the square.

 Fig. 20

You can increase your skill in this activity with the following game.
*OBS 3.
Aim of the Game: To make the closest estimate of the number of dots.
Number of Players: Two or more.
Materials Needed: Pencils and paper.
How to Play: Each player draws at least twenty dots inside the same square. Each player then has five seconds to look at the square, and guess the total number of dots inside it. The guesses are written down. The dots are then counted, and the player who is closest (above or below the actual total) wins.
Variation: Use a circle or irregular closed figure, instead of a square.
Variation: Everything the same, except the player who is closest without going over the total wins. Any player who guesses more than the total loses.

As a strategy, you could
— imagine the square divided into four quadrants (Fig. 21),
— estimate or count the number of dots in one quadrant, and
— multiply that number by four.

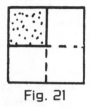

Fig. 21

The Number of Objects You Imagine

In this next activity, you must estimate how many objects of a known size will fit into a given space. You may do this yourself (how close can you come?), or as a game with others (who can come the closest?).

* **OBS 4.**

Aim of the Game: To make the closest estimate of the number of mosaic pieces that will fit into an area without overlap.

Number of Players: One or more.

Materials Needed: Pencil and paper.

How to Play: Draw a rectangle of unknown size. Trace the outline of one mosaic somewhere inside the rectangle as a model (Fig. 22a). Each player then writes down an estimate of the total number of mosaic pieces that will fit inside the rectangle. Pieces may touch but not overlap.

Fill the rectangle with mosaic pieces and count them. The player who is closest (above or below the actual total) wins (Fig. 22b).

Variation: Use any irregular figure, instead of a rectangle (Fig. 22c).

Variation: Use dominoes, straight trominoes or right trominoes instead of mosaic pieces.

Variation: Use a coin instead of mosaic pieces.

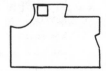

Fig. 22a   **Fig. 22b**   **Fig. 22c**

As a strategy, playing with the rectangle,
— try to imagine how many mosaic pieces will fit across the top of
the rectangle, and
— how many will fit down the side.
— Then multiply these two numbers.

The Areas You See

In this next section, you must make estimates about areas you see. We begin with the simple judgment of *more* or *less*: Does Fig. 23 have more black or more white?

Fig. 23

Here is a game that will help improve your ability to make this kind of estimate.
* **OBS 5.**
Aim of the Game: To guess correctly whether a square has more white or black area.
Number of Players: Two.
Materials Needed: 5x5 grid; mosaic pieces.
How to Play: Player A fills the grid with mosaic pieces so that a total of 15 of the 25 squares are of one color (black or white), and 10 of the other. Some individual squares may be half black and half white; it is the total that counts. Player B looks at the mosaic for five seconds, and estimates whether there is more black or white in it. Player B is told whether he/she is right or wrong. The players switch roles.
Variation: Fill the grid with 14 of one color, 11 of the other.
Variation: Fill a 6x6 grid with 7 white and 29 black, or with 11 white and 25 black squares. Player B must estimate whether grid is less or more than one quarter white.
Variation: Use a non-rectangular outline, as in Fig. 24.
Variation: Fill up the grid by chance, and play by yourself, or with each player independently guessing whether there is more white or black.

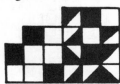
Fig. 24

Here are some hints for a strategy to use in playing this game:

— If the total mosaic is symmetrical, look at only one-half or one-quarter of it. Count how many white, and multiply by two (or by four).

— If not, go row by row, as time permits.

— Disregard any tile that is half white and half black.

Solutions

Page 80

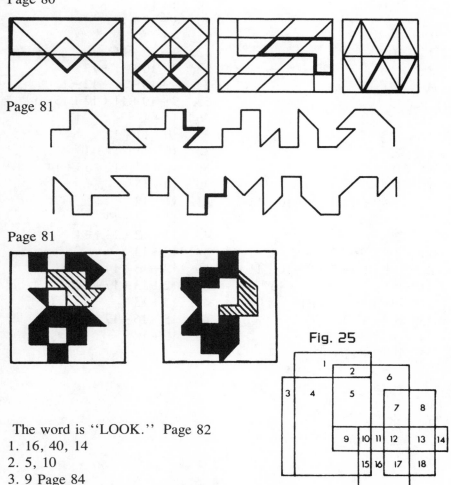

Page 81

Page 81

Fig. 25

The word is "LOOK." Page 82

1. 16, 40, 14
2. 5, 10
3. 9 Page 84

4. Here's a systematic way to count the rectangles:

    a. Give each separate area a number, as in Fig. 25.

    b. Starting with area number 1, list each area that by itself is a rectangle (Numbers 1 to 14 in the listing that follows).

c.   Starting with area number 1, list each combination of areas that forms a rectangle (Numbers 15 to 49 below). Remember that two or more areas that together form a rectangle can be listed in any order, so don't list the same combination more than once. For example, after you list area 1 + area 2, don't later list area 2 + area 1.

1.	2	26.	7 + 8
2.	3	27.	7 + 8 + 12 + 13
3.	5	28.	7 + 8 + 12 + 13 + 17 + 18
4.	7	29.	8 + 13
5.	8	30.	8 + 13 + 18
6.	9	31.	9 + 10
7.	10	32.	9 + 10 + 11
8.	11	33.	9 + 10 + 11 + 12
9.	12	34.	9 + 10 + 11 + 12 + 13
10.	13	35.	9 + 10 + 11 + 12 + 13 + 14
11.	14	36.	10 + 11
12.	15	37.	10 + 11 + 12
13.	17	38.	10 + 11 + 12 + 13
14.	18	39.	10 + 11 + 12 + 13 + 14
15.	1 + 2	40.	10 + 15
16.	1 + 2 + 4 + 5 + 9 + 10 + 15	41.	11 + 12
17.	2 + 5	42.	11 + 12 + 13
18.	2 + 5 + 9 + 10	43.	11 + 12 + 13 + 14
19.	2 + 5 + 6 + 7	44.	12 + 13
20.	2 + 5 + 6 + 7 + 9 + 10 + 11 + 12	45.	12 + 13 + 14
21.	3 + 4 + 5 + 9 + 10 + 15	46.	12 + 13 + 17 + 18
22.	4 + 5 + 9 + 10 + 15	47.	13 + 18
23.	5 + 9 + 10	48.	15 + 16 + 17
24.	6 + 7	49.	17 + 18
25.	6 + 7 + 11 + 12		

	Page 121	Page 122
1.	3243	
2.	26	37
3.	22	22
4.	7	4
5.	3	6
6.	3	1
7.	1	0
8.	0	0
9.	-	0

CHAPTER VIII

IMAGING CHANGES

To imagine what something would look like if changed is an important visual skill.
— If you are purchasing a new sofa, you want to visualize what it will look like in your living room.
— If you are purchasing a shirt, you want to visualize how well it would go with the pants you have home.
— If a part of your car engine breaks off, you want to be able to see how and where it was attached.
— An archeologist tries to imagine a whole bowl from a clay fragment.
You have already worked on this skill in earlier chapters:
— In the Mosaics chapter you imagined what a design would look like
  — if black and white were reversed.
  — if it were rotated 90 degrees one or more times.
  — if it were flipped over.
— In the polynominoes chapter you imagined what a pentomino would look like if flipped over.
Now in this chapter we will pay attention to some other changes that involve *three* dimensions, such as:
— seeing objects in a new position;
— folding a paper to form a three-dimensional object;
— folding, cutting and unfolding a paper; and

Imagining Letters Move

Suppose the letters "AB" were on a thin piece of paper, hinged to the table on its right side, as shown in Fig. 1a. If you flipped the paper over (Fig. 1b), what would the letters look like?
Fig. 1c shows you. If the paper in Fig. 1c were now hinged on its bottom

side and flipped over, what would the letters look like? Fig. 1d shows you. Finally, if the paper in Fig. 1d were now hinged on its left side and flipped over, what would the letters look like? Fig. 1e shows you. Fig. 1f shows you the results of all three flips at a glance.

Now try to see how the letters in Figs. 1g, 1h and 1i would look if flipped over three times this way. Draw them. Then place each set of letters on a separate sheet of paper, turn the paper and check to see if your drawings are correct. Another way to check your drawings is to place a mirror where the imaginary hinge is, as in Fig. 1j.

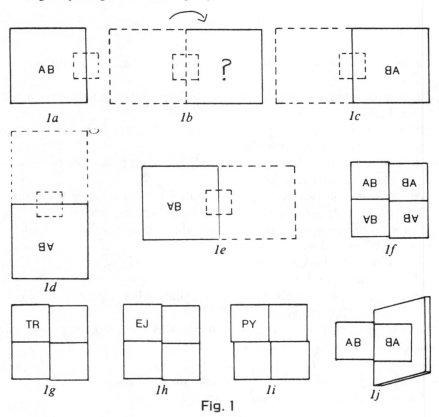

Fig. 1

Folding a Paper to Form a Three-Dimensional Object

The Cube

A cube is a simple three-dimensional object we can make by folding a paper. If you fold Fig. 2a along the dotted lines, you will get a cube (Fig. 2b).

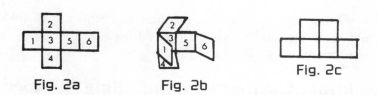

Fig. 2a   Fig. 2b   Fig. 2c

But not every arrangement of six boxes that are connected together by common sides can be folded to form a cube. The boxes in Fig. 2c cannot.

See if you can tell which of the arrangements in Fig. 3 can and which cannot be folded into a cube.

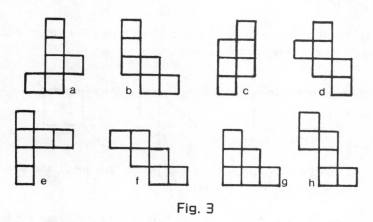

Fig. 3

If you are not sure about a particular arrangement, draw it on a piece of paper, cut it out, and fold it.

The Pyramid with a Triangular Base

The pyramid is another simple three-dimensional object we can make by folding a paper. This object has four triangular sides. We can form a pyramid from four triangles connected by common sides. As you may remember from the Polynominoes chapter, four triangles can be connected together in only three different ways (Fig. 4a).

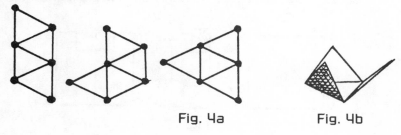

Fig. 4a   Fig. 4b

See if you can imagine which of these arrangements can be folded into a pyramid, as in Fig. 4b, before you read further.

Only the one in the middle cannot.

Folding, Cutting and Unfolding a Paper

In this next section we will fold a paper, then make cuts in it so that the cuts will appear in certain positions when the paper is again unfolded.

Types of Cuts.

We begin with a square piece of paper. If your paper is longer than it is wide, Fig. 5 shows how to make it square.

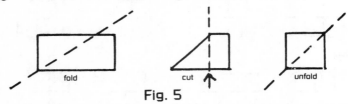

Fig. 5

I.   In the simplest case, you fold the paper just once, and cut out a symmetric piece before you unfold it.

    1.   Fold the square paper evenly from left to right, cut out a small square from the upper right, and unfold the paper (Fig. 6).

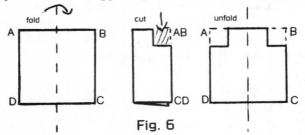

Fig. 6

    2.   Fold the square paper evenly from left to right, cut out a small square from the upper left, and unfold the paper (Fig. 7).

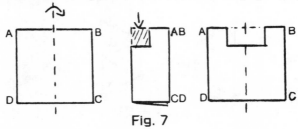

Fig. 7

3. Fold the square paper evenly from top to bottom, cut out a small square from the lower right, and unfold the paper (Fig. 8). The result is like Fig. 6 rotated 90 degrees clockwise.

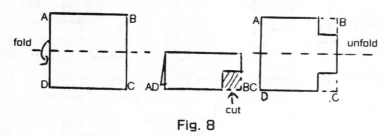

Fig. 8

4. Fold the square paper evenly diagonally. By cutting in different locations, you can get the results of Figs. 9a, 9b, and 9c.

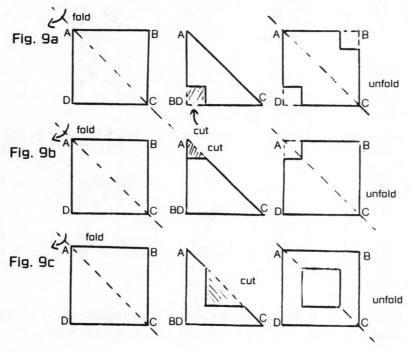

II. Here's a slightly more complicated situation. Fold the square paper evenly from left to right, make *two* symmetrical cuts, and unfold the paper (Figs. 10a, 10b, 10c).

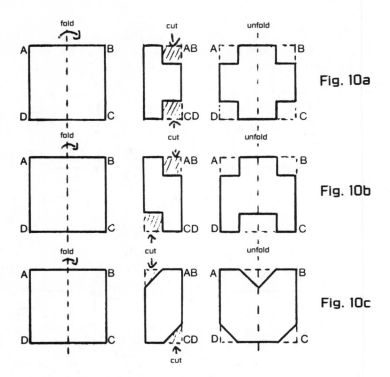

Fig. 10a

Fig. 10b

Fig. 10c

III.   Here's an even more complicated situation. Fold the paper twice before cutting, as in Fig. 11.

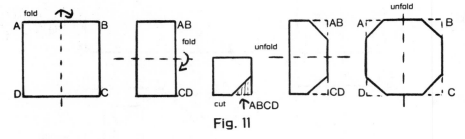

Fig. 11

IV.   Finally, even if you cut off a *non*-symmetrical piece, as in Fig. 12, when you unfold your paper you will have a symmetrical figure.

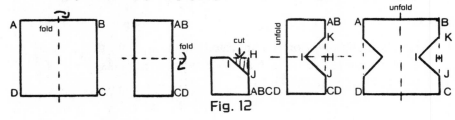

Fig. 12

The first unfolding will show a triangular-shaped piece missing, twice the size of triangle IJH. Its sides will be
— IJ
— IK, where K is the same distance from H that J is.
— JK (Fig. 12d).
The next unfolding will show the same shape piece that is missing on the right side will also be missing (flipped over) on the left.
— If the cut in the double-folded paper had been made as in Fig. 13c, the unfolded result would be as shown in Fig. 13e.

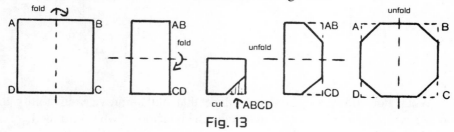

Fig. 13

　　　Try different ways of folding and cutting paper, and seeing what results you get.

Problems to Solve

We will now present two kinds of problems to solve:
— In the first, we show you how the paper was folded and cut. Draw what the paper will look like when completely unfolded in each case of Fig. 14.

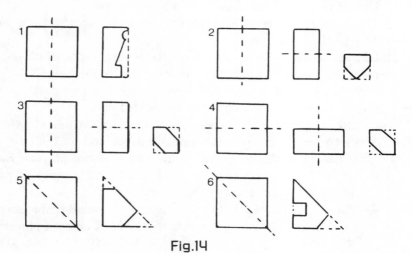

Fig.14

—In the second kind of problem, we show you what a paper looks like after being folded, cut and unfolded. Draw how it was folded and cut in each case of Fig. 15.

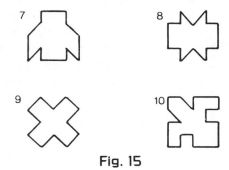

Fig. 15

When you are ready, here is a game that will improve your ability to make cuts in a folded paper that will match a given model when unfolded.

*IMAG 1.

Aim of the Game: To cut a folded paper so that it matches a given model when unfolded.

Number of Players: Two.

Materials Needed: Square pieces of paper at least 4 x 4; scissors.

How to Play:

a.   With the other player not looking, fold a square piece of paper in half twice as shown in Fig. 16a or 16b.

b.   Cut out a section of the folded paper.

c.   Unfold the paper and show it to the other player.

d.   The other player now takes another piece of paper to fold, cut, and unfold to get the same result.

Unfold the second paper; if it matches the model, the other player A gets one point. If it doesn't, you get one point.

Then switch roles with the other player. A total of five points wins.

Variation: Cut out *two* sections from the folded paper.

Variation: Fold the paper one or two times; cut as many times as you want. Don't tell the other player how many times the paper has been folded or cut.

Note: This game can also be played with more than two players. Either

— each of the others must try to fold and cut a piece of paper to reach the same result as the model, or

— Player A presents a pattern for Player B, Player B presents a pattern for Player C, Player C for Player D, etc. Then each player must try to cut and fold a piece of paper to match the model given to him/her.

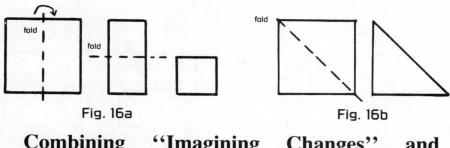

Fig. 16a   Fig. 16b

Combining "Imagining Changes" and "Polynominoes"

Here's a chance to combine what you've learned about polynominoes and imagining changes. In this chapter, you learned that you could fold certain arrangements of six connected squares to form a square. In the Polynominoes chapter you learned that a pentomino is an arrangement of five connected squares. Which pentominoes could be folded to form an "open" cube with one surface missing?

The Continuous Path Puzzle

You can draw some figures in a continuous path, that is, *without going over the same line twice and without taking your pencil off the paper.* With others, you cannot. Why?

— You obviously can do this with a circle, no matter where you start (Fig. 17).
— With some other figures, it depends on where you start. You can draw Fig. 18 in a continuous path only if you begin your path at a point where the circle meets the straight line.
— Still other figures you cannot draw in a continuous path no matter where you start (Fig. 19).

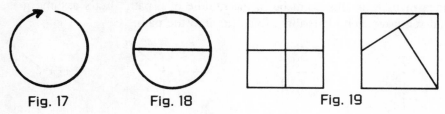

Fig. 17   Fig. 18   Fig. 19

See which of the figures below you can draw in a continuous path (Fig. 20).

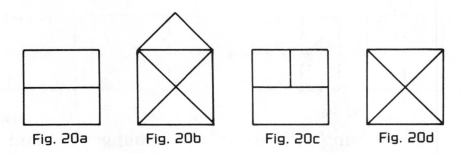

Fig. 20a   Fig. 20b   Fig. 20c   Fig. 20d

Then try to discover what they have in common, and what the others have in common, before you read further.

Figs. 20a and 20b can be drawn in a continuous path, as shown in Fig. 21a and 21b.

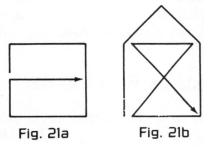

Fig. 21a   Fig. 21b

Each has no more than two points where three lines meet.

Figs. 20c and 20d *cannot* be drawn in a continuous path. Each has more than two points where three lines meet.

In general *you cannot draw a continuous path when a figure has more than two points at which three lines meet.* Let's see why this is so.

A point on a path must be either the starting point, some point in the middle, or the end point of that path. Fig. 22a shows a point where three lines meet. Can this point be in the middle of a path? Let's assume it is, and see how each of its three lines fits into the path.

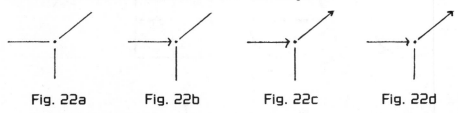

Fig. 22a   Fig. 22b   Fig. 22c   Fig. 22d

a.   We place a "1" on one line to show how the path first comes toward the point (Fig. 22b).

b.   We then place a "2" on a second line to show the path away from the point (Fig. 22c).

c.   We place a "3" on the third line to show a return path to the point (Fig. 22d).

d.   But the path must now end at the point, since there are no further lines to or from the point.

e.   We conclude that the point in Fig. 22a where three lines meet cannot be a point in the middle of the path.

f.   It must be either the starting point or the end point of a path.

In general when a path has two points where three lines meet, then one must be the starting point and the other the end point of the path.

Now we can see the problem when a figure has more than two points at which three lines meet.

— One point could be the starting point for a path,

— A second point could be the end point,

— But the third point cannot be the starting point, a middle point, or the end point. It is left out.

So it is *impossible* to draw such a figure in a continuous path.

We see now why certain figures (with more than two points where three lines meet) cannot be drawn in a continuous path. But the rule is more general than that: Figures that have more than two points where an odd number of lines meet cannot be drawn in a continuous path.

We see the importance of odd-even in path puzzles.

Another Path Problem

Look now at Fig. 23a. Can you start at point A, pass through each circle just once, travelling along the dotted lines, and end up at Z? Try this before you read the explanation.

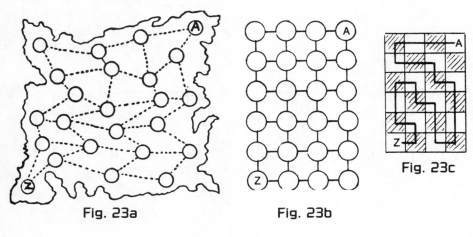

Fig. 23a   Fig. 23b   Fig. 23c

a. We can simplify the diagram by straightening out the locations of the circles, as in Fig. 23b.

b. Next we can change the circles to boxes, and color in every alternate circle in a checkerboard fashion, as in Fig. 23c.

c. Now we can use the odd-even principle. You must make 23 moves to get from A to Z.

d. But each odd-numbered move is into a black circle, and Z is white.

e. So you cannot arrive at Z on the last (23rd) move, no matter what route you take.

Solutions

Page 97

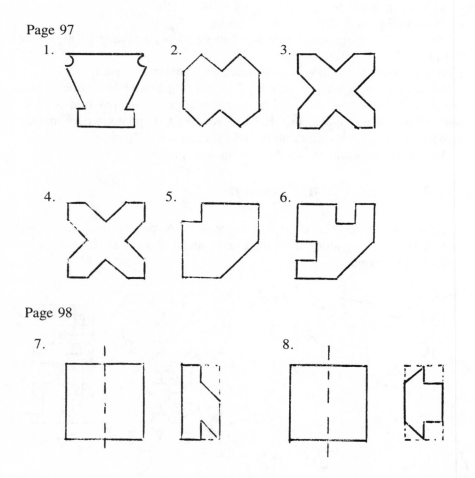

Page 98

9.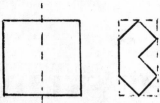

10.

CHAPTER IX

TOPOLOGY: THE STUDY OF CONNECTIONS

This chapter deals with what's connected with what, not with the distance between this and that, or with the size or shape of things. The mathematical word for this topic is *topology*. But you don't need any special background in mathematics to enjoy the activities we present here.

In this chapter we will give you a deeper understanding of what topology is, show you some topological games to play with your friends, show you a topological trick to amaze your friends, give you some topological puzzles, and show you some practical situations where you can apply topology.

Connections Between Two Regions

Suppose we draw a square on a rubber sheet, and then divide the square into two regions, A and B, as in Fig. 1a.

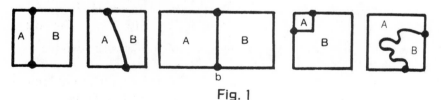

Fig. 1

A and B share a border. We can stretch the rubber sheet in many ways, as in Figs. 1b through 1e. No matter how we stretch the sheet, regions A and B will still share a border, and a point inside region A will never touch a point inside region B. Only the sizes and shapes of regions A and B will change. In terms of *topology*, we say that all the diagrams in Fig. 1 are identical! By this we mean

- We can turn any of the diagrams into any other by stretching the same sheet.
- In each diagram, regions A and B will always share a border.
- In each diagram a point in region A will never touch a point in region B.
- In terms of topology, the sizes and shapes of these diagrams don't matter.

By contrast, suppose that we drew regions A and B on other rubber sheets as shown in Figs. 2 and 3. Then, no matter how we stretched the sheets,
— in Fig. 2, all points in region A will always be inside region B also.
— in Fig. 3, region A and region B will only be connected at one point, and never share a common border.

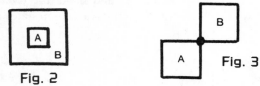

Fig. 2   Fig. 3

In terms of topology, then, we say that Figs. 2 and 3 are different from each other, and each is different from all the diagrams of Fig. 1.

Dividing a Shape into Three Regions

Let's see now what happens if we divide a square (or any other closed figure) into *three* regions, A, B and C. In terms of topology, here are some different ways the three regions could be connected:

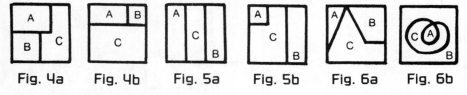

Fig. 4a   Fig. 4b   Fig. 5a   Fig. 5b   Fig. 6a   Fig. 6b

— Each region shares a common border with each of the other two regions (Figs. 4a and 4b).
— Two regions A and B each shares a common border with a third region (C), but do not share a common border with each other (Figs. 5a and 5b).
— Two regions A and B each share a common border with region C, and do not share a common border with each other. All three regions meet in a point (Fig. 6a and 6b).

Imagine each diagram in Figs. 4, 5 and 6 drawn on a rubber sheet.

We can stretch Fig. 4a into Fig. 4b, or Fig. 5a into Fig. 5b, or Fig. 6a into Fig. 6b. But we cannot, for example, stretch Fig. 4a into Figs. 5a, 5b, 6a or 6b.

In general, when we draw a figure with several regions on a rubber sheet, no matter how we stretch the sheet,

- regions that share a common border will still share a common border, and
- regions that do not share a common border will remain that way.

Maps Divided into Many Regions

Fig. 7a is a map of Australia, divided into its six states. Imagine it drawn on a rubber sheet. By stretching the sheet, we can smooth the curves (Fig. 7b), replace them with straight lines and make the overall shape a square (Fig. 7c). Now we see the topology of the Australian states in a simple form.

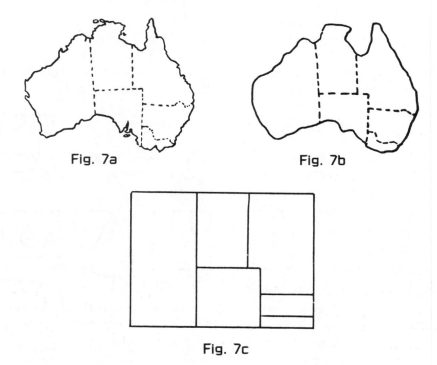

Fig. 7a   Fig. 7b

Fig. 7c

Activities

1. Reduce the outline maps in Fig. 8 of Canada, South America, and Western Europe to show the topology of the countries in a simple squared-off form, as we have done with the states of Australia.

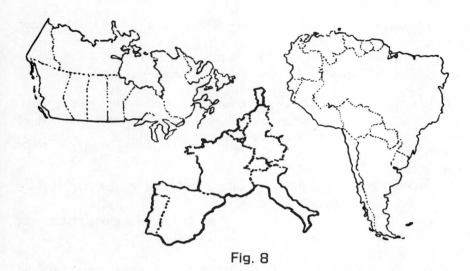

Fig. 8

2. In terms of topology, is the figure on the left in Fig. 9 the same as A, B, C or D on the right?

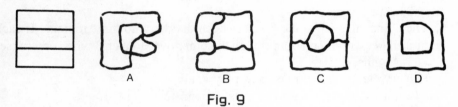

A   B   C   D

Fig. 9

3. In terms of topology, is the figure on the left in Fig. 10 the same as A, B, C or D on the right?

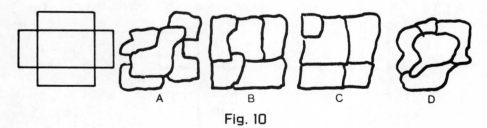

A   B   C   D

Fig. 10

4. Make up puzzles like those in (2) and (3) above for your friend to solve. Have your friend make up this kind of puzzle for you.

Games

The Three Region Game

Here is a game in which the players divide a square into three regions. One player tries to make each region share a common border with both of the other regions, and the other player tries to prevent this.
*TOPO 1.
Aim of the Game:
— For Player B, to divide the square into three regions that all share common borders with each other.
— For Player A, to divide the square into three regions that do not all share common borders with each other.
Number of Players: Two.
Materials Needed: Grid of dots 4x4 on a piece of graph paper with the outside borders drawn; pencil.
How to Play: Players alternate turns. Player A starts. On each turn a player makes a horizontal or vertical connection between two dots, or one dot and the adjacent border.
The game ends when the grid has been divided into three regions. If each region shares a common border with the other two, Player B wins; otherwise, Player A wins.
Players then reverse roles, and play again.
Variation: Start with a grid of dots 4x5, instead of 4x4.
Variation: Start with a grid of dots 5x5, instead of 4x4.
Fig. 11 shows some sample games. In the first and third sample games, the three regions do not all share common borders. A wins. In the second sample game, the three regions all have common borders. B wins.

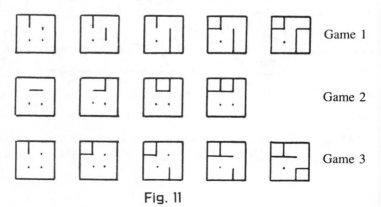

Game 1

Game 2

Game 3

Fig. 11

Note that in the third sample game the middle region contains one extra line. One end of this line is "loose," so it does not form a border. There are still only three regions in the square.

Improving Your Skill in the Three Region Game

Here now are some game situations where you must choose the best move to make. For each situation,
— choose the move that wins for you immediately, or
— wins for you on later moves no matter what your opponent does.
We have given each possible connection a number, as shown in Figs. 12a and 12b.
— Use the numbers in Fig. 12a to describe your next move in situations 1,2,6 and 7.
— Use the number in Fig. 12b to describe your next move in situations 3, 4,5,8,9 and 10.
Write down the number of the winning moves you have chosen. Answers are given at the end of the chapter; in some cases, there may be other correct answers.

Fig. 12a   Fig. 12b

I.   You are Player A; you want the three regions to not all have common borders.

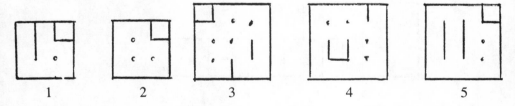

1   2   3   4   5

II.   You are Player B; you want all three regions to have common borders.

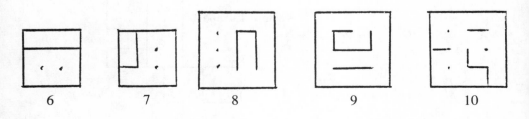

6   7   8   9   10

I.   Your strategy as Player A:

If the grid has already been divided into two regions that share a common border (examples 1, 2, 3 and 5), find a way to subdivide the larger region by a line that doesn't touch the smaller region. In example 1, line #10 will accomplish this; line #8 will not, because it will touch the smaller region.

If the grid has not already been subdivided (example 4), try to subdivide it into a very large and very small region. Then you will be able to further subdivide the larger region without touching the smaller region.

II.   Your strategy as Player B:

If the grid has already been subdivided into two regions that share a common border, try to subdivide the smaller region (if it has at least two squares). In example 6, you could subdivide the smaller region by line #1 or line #2.

A General Principle in Topology

You have learned a powerful general principle: Drawings that look very different from each other can be similar in terms of topology.

Solutions

Page 107

Canada

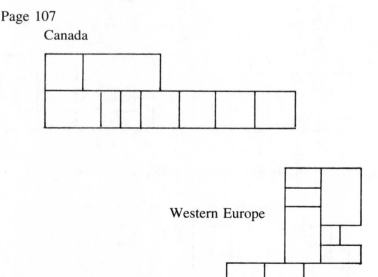

Western Europe

South America

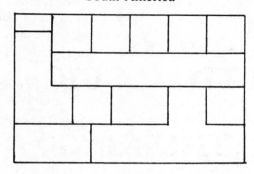

2. B
3. A

Page 109
1. 5, 7 or 10
2. 5, then 10
3. 10, then 22
4. 16, then 18
5. 18, then 14

6. 1 or 2
7. 13
8. 19, then 23
9. 15, then 5
10. 24, then 11

CHAPTER X

DEDUCTIVE LOGIC AND VISUAL THINKING

Deductive logic deals with putting together related facts to reach a conclusion that must be so. We have already made use of deductive logic
— in the Polynominoes chapter when we considered whether we could fill a grid with dominoes:
— If each domino covers two boxes, and
— a 3x3 grid contains nine boxes, and
— nine is an odd number,
— then we cannot fill a 3x3 grid with dominoes.
— in the Topology chapter when we considered going through every box in a grid once to get from A to B:
— If on every move you go from a white to black box or from a black to a white box, and
— You start in A, a white box and want to go to B, a white box on your 15th move, then you cannot do it.

In this chapter we show you
— how to bring together related facts in a "20 Questions" game format to eliminate all but one of a set of polynominoes or mosaics.
— how to use the Venn diagram as a visual tool in working out problems of deductive logic.

Finding One of Many

In the well-known game "20 Questions," one player tries to discover what person, place, or thing another player has in mind by asking as few questions as possible, each of which can be answered by "yes" or "no."

You can play this same game with visual objects, instead of people or places. Doing so will strengthen your abilities to observe differences among objects, see similarities among objects, form categories of objects, and put into words what these categories are.

Here is how the game might be played.

* DED 1.

Aim of the Game: To discover the secret polynomino piece.

Number of Players: Two.

Materials Needed: One of each polynomino piece: 1 monomino, one domino, 2 trominoes, and 12 pentominoes, for a total of 21 objects. 21 objects.

How to Play: Player A lays out all 21 pieces on the table, and draws one of them (the "secret piece") on a piece of paper kept out of Player B's view. All 21 pieces are laid out on the table. Player B asks a question about the secret piece which can be answered by "yes" or "no" only. Player B cannot move the pieces around into groups or point to pieces; each question must be clearly stated in words.

After getting an answer from Player A, Player B removes those pieces that can be eliminated. The game continues in the same way with further questions and answers until Player B discovers the secret piece.

Player A receives one point for each question Player B has asked. Then the players switch roles. After each player has had an equal number of turns in each role, the player with more points wins.

Variation: Include hexominoes and hexiamonds, as well as the polynominoes.

Variation: Make up your own figures to use in this game, instead of the polynomino pieces. Draw each figure on a grid of dots with connected horizontal, vertical, and/or diagonal lines (Fig. 1). Each player contributes half of them.

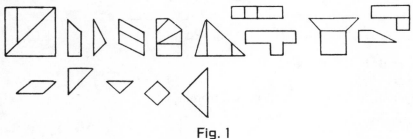

Fig. 1

Here's how a game might go, starting with all the polynomino pieces (Fig. 2a).

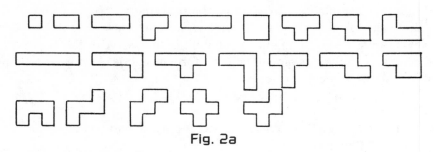

Fig. 2a

Player B: Is the secret piece made up of five squares?
Player A: No.
   Player B removes all the pentominoes, leaving the pieces shown in Fig 2b.

Fig. 2b

Player B: Is it a rectangle?
Player A: No.
   Player B removes all rectangles, leaving the pieces shown in Fig 2c.

Fig. 2c

Player B: Is it symmetrical?
Player A: Yes.
   Player B removes the non-symmetrical objects, leaving the pieces shown in Fig. 2d.

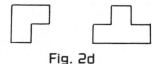

Fig. 2d

Player B: Is it L-shaped?
Player A: No.
Player B: It must be this T-shaped tromino.

Player A: Yes.

A good strategy for this game is to ask questions that will eliminate about half the possibilities, whether the answer is "yes" or "no." Since you begin with 21 pieces, the best first question will divide the objects into groups of 11 and 10. Can you think of such a question?

Here are some:

— Can the object fit inside a 2x3 grid? (Fig. 3).

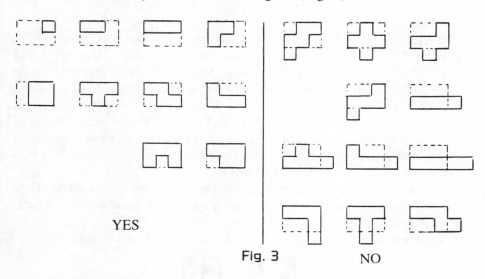

YES

Fig. 3   NO

— Does it have more than six sides? (Fig. 4).

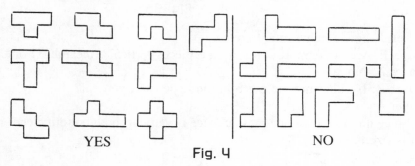

YES   NO

Fig. 4

Activity

Suppose you were using a set of figures with which to play the second variation of this game. Think of a question that could eliminate half the figures at the start for the set of figures in Fig. 1.

Here are some possibilities:

(a) Does it have diagonal lines?

(b)   Can you draw it in one continuous stroke, without taking your pencil off the paper and without retracing?

Do these possibilities work?

Here's another game that helps you to formulate questions and put together the facts you get to eliminate all but one possibility.

*DED 2.

Aim of the Game: To discover the orientations of four mosaic pieces attached together in the form of a square.

Number of Players: Two.

Materials Needed: Four identical mosaic pieces; pencil and paper.

How to Play: Player A secretly places the four mosaic pieces in a 2x2 square (as in Fig. 5a or 5b) kept out of Player B's view. Player B asks a question about the secret arrangement of the pieces that can only be answered by ''yes'' or ''no'' only.

After getting an answer from Player A, Player B may makes notes to keep track of what possibilities have been eliminated. The game continues in the same way with further questions and answers until Player B discovers the arrangement of the four secret pieces.

Player A receives one point for each question Player B has asked. Then the players switch roles. After each player has had an equal number of turns in each role, the player with more points wins.

Variation: Use a mixture of ▯ and ◩, instead of four identical pieces.

Fig. 5a    Fig. 5b

Here's how a game might go:

Player B: Are two or more of the mosaic pieces vertical? (meaning ▯ or ▮).
Player A: No.
Player B: Is either mosaic piece in the upper part vertical?
Player A: Yes.

Since no more than one mosaic piece is vertical, both bottom pieces must be horizontal.

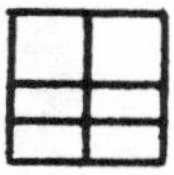

Player B: Is it the one on the left?
Player A: No.

So it must be the one on the right that is vertical.

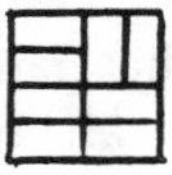

Player B: In the vertical piece, is the black side on the left?
Player A: Yes.

Player B: Do the two pieces on the bottom have the same orientation?
Player A: Yes.
Player B: Black on top?
Player A: No.

Player B: Does the upper left piece have the same orientation as the lower left piece?
Player A: No.
Player B: Then it must be like this:

Player A: Yes.

Notice that you can get as much information from a "no" answer as from a "yes" answer.

Here's still another game that helps you to formulate questions and put together the facts you get to eliminate all but one possibility.

*DED 3.

Aim of the Game: To locate the treasure hidden in one square of the grid.

Number of Players: Two.

Materials Needed: Grid 6x6; paper and pencil; mosaic tiles.

Preparation: Player A secretly writes down the coordinates of the one grid square containing the treasure.

How to Play: The grid is filled with mosaic tiles. On each turn Player B asks a question about the location of the treasure which Player A answers with a "yes" or "no." After each question Player B removes tiles from those squares the answer indicates do not contain the treasure. Game continues until the treasure is discovered. Then the players' roles are reversed. Player who requires fewer questions to locate the treasure wins.

Variation: Use an 8x8 grid.

Variation: Use a treasure that lies in three squares connected as a tromino (Fig. 6). Player A answers "yes" if any part of the treasure is in the area asked about.

Fig. 7 shows a sample game.

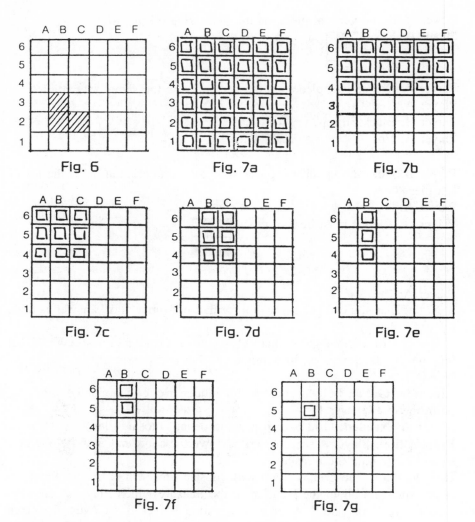

Fig. 6 Fig. 7a Fig. 7b

Fig. 7c Fig. 7d Fig. 7e

Fig. 7f Fig. 7g

Is the treasure in the upper half of the grid? Yes. (Fig. 7b)
In the right half? No. (Fig. 7c)
In column A? No. (Fig. 7d)
In column B? Yes. (Fig. 7e)
In row 4? No. (Fig. 7f)
In row 5? Yes. (Fig. 7g)
The treasure must be in B5. You're right.

*DED 4.

Aim of the Game: To find some secret mosaic pieces out of many (3 out of 5), by choosing which pieces you want to get information about.

Number of Players: Two.

Materials Needed: The 88 mosaic pieces (five different kinds); red tokens (or pennies or buttons).

How to Play: Player A chooses three *different* mosaic pieces to be the secret pieces, and puts them face down in a row. Player B chooses three other pieces to get information about, and places them face up in a row below the secret pieces. A places one red token alongside this row for each mosaic piece that is the same as one of the secret pieces. In this game, the orientation of the piece does not matter. For example, ◨ is the same as ◧.

The game continues, with B choosing further rows and A giving information, until B finds out what the three secret mosaic pieces are. Then the two players switch roles; B chooses three secret mosaic pieces, and A must find them out.

The player choosing the secret pieces receives one point for each row the player finding them out needs. Play three, five or ten rounds. The player with more total points wins.

Variation: The three secret mosaic pieces do *not* have to be different from each other.

Here's an example of the game, played under the condition that the three secret pieces *are* different from each other.

At the beginning, these are all the possibilities for what the three secret pieces are:

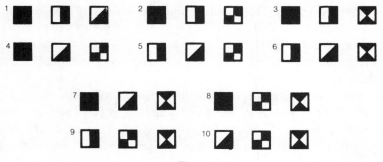

Fig. 8

Player B picks a ■, ◨, and a ◪ for his first row, and Player A puts down one token. This means that one of those in the row asked about (and only one!) is a secret mosaic piece. B can eliminate all the possibilities that contain more than one of ■, ◨, and ◪. This leaves just:

Now B picks ■, ▨, ☒ to ask about in his second row, and A puts down *two* tokens. B can eliminate the very row asked about (because A didn't put down *three* tokens) This leaves:

Now B tries ◤, ▨, ☒, and A puts down two tokens. Again B can eliminate the row just asked about (because A didn't put down *three* tokens), and the secret pieces must be ◻, ▨, ☒. Since B needed three rows of information, A gets three points.

*DED 5.

Aim of the Game: To find some secret mosaic pieces out of many (3 out of 5) and their positions, by choosing which pieces you want to get information about.

Number of Players: Two.

Materials Needed: The 88 mosaic pieces (five different kinds); red tokens (or pennies or buttons).

How to Play: Player A chooses three *different* mosaic pieces to be the secret pieces, and puts them face down in a row. Player B chooses three pieces to get information about, and places them face up in a row below the secret pieces. A places one green token alongside this row for each mosaic piece that is the same as one of the secret pieces *and is in the same position* (left, middle or right) as that secret piece, and one red token alongside this row for each mosaic piece that is the same as one of the secret pieces but not in the same position as it.

In this game, the *orientation* of the piece does not matter. For example, ◻, is the same as ◧.

The game continues, with B choosing further rows and A giving information, until B finds out what the three secret mosaic pieces are and what positions they are in. Then the two players switch roles; B chooses three secret mosaic pieces, and A must find out what they are and where they are.

The player choosing the secret pieces receives one point for each row the player finding them out needs. Play three, five or ten rounds. The player with more total points wins.

Variation: The three secret mosaic pieces *do not* have to be different from each other.

Here are some examples to get you acquainted with how the green and red tokens are used in this more complicated situation:

Secret Pieces: ■▨◻   Here the green token shows there is a ■
First Row: ■☒◤ g   in both the secret pieces and in the first row, in the same position (on the left) in both.

Secret Pieces:	■ ⊡ ☐
First Row:	◿ ☒ ■ r

Here the red token shows there is a ■ in both the secret pieces and in the first row, but on the left in one case, and on the right in the other.

Secret Pieces:	■ ⊡ ☐
First Row:	⊡ ◿ ■ rr

Here two red tokens shows there are a ■ and a ⊡ in both the secret pieces and in the first row, but they are not in the same position in both.

Secret Pieces:	■ ☐ ☐
First Row:	⊡ ◿ ☐ gr

Here the one green and one red token show that the ⊡ and the ☐ are in both the secret pieces and in the first row, but only the ☐ is in the same position (on the right).

Secret Pieces:	■ ⊡ ☐
First Row:	⊡ ■ ☐ grr

Here the one green and two red tokens show that all the first row pieces are secret pieces, but only the ☐ is in the same position.

*DED 6.

Aim of the Game: To find out the secret digit.
Number of Players: Two.
Materials Needed: Pencil and paper.
How to Play: Player A writes a secret digit from 0 to 9. Player B asks whether a particular set of coordinates for the secret digit, as it is drawn in Fig. 9, contains a dot.

For example, "Is there a dot at D2?"
— If the secret digit is 0, 1, 2, 3 or 7, Player A will reply, "Yes."
— If the secret digit is 4, 5, 6, 8 or 9, Player A will reply, "No."

The game continues until Player B eliminates all but the secret digit. Then the two players switch roles; B chooses the secret digit, and A must find it out.

The player choosing the secret digit receives one point for each set of coordinates the other player asks about. Play three, five or ten rounds. The player with more total points wins.

Variation: Instead of a digit, Player A chooses a secret letter, as it is drawn in Fig. 10.

Variation: Player A chooses either a secret digit, as drawn in Fig. 9, or a secret letter, as drawn in Fig. 10.

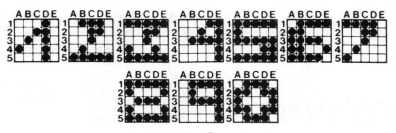

Fig. 9

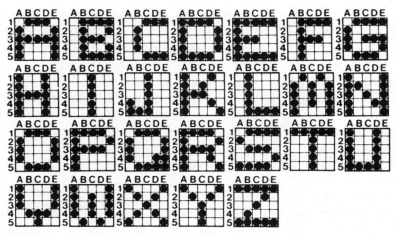

Fig. 10

From the deductive logic games we have presented, you can learn the following general principles:

— List all the possibilities in the situation.
— Think of ways to get information that will reduce the possibilities in half, whether the answer is "yes" or "no."
— Remember that you can get as much information from a "no" answer as from a "yes" answer.
— Find an effective way to keep track of the information you get.

CHAPTER XI

INDUCTIVE LOGIC

Inductive logic deals with finding out from a number of examples what is true *in general*. By noticing that a toothpick floats, a wooden chair floats, a log floats, and a wooden bookcase floats, we might make the generalization that wooden objects float. This would be a rule of nature. Another rule of nature we might arrive at through observation is that magnets attract iron.

There are also rules for operating effectively: avoid certain routes during rush hour; do not exercise strenuously right after eating.

We discover these rules by putting our experiences together to see what is similar among different events. This process is called using inductive logic: reasoning from particular facts to a general conclusion. In this chapter we practice the skill of using inductive logic with visual materials.

This chapter deals with several kinds of rules:

— a simple *sequence* rule for arranging figures in a row from left to right.

— a more complicated sequence rule in arranging them from left to right *and* from top to bottom.

— the rule for which figures belong in a category and which do not
 — when a single factor is involved, and
 — when two factors are involved.

All these rules are frequently found in intelligence tests. We give you practice in recognizing them through puzzles and games. Then we provide some games to help you recognize an entire mosaic pattern or photograph from seeing pieces of it.

Sequence

One Factor

Increasing or decreasing amounts.

As a child you may have "lined up in size place" in your classroom. The shortest kid was at the head of the line, then the next shortest, and so on, with the tallest kid at the rear of the line. This is an example of arranging a series of objects in a sequence according to a rule.

To "line up in size place" we pay attention only to height, and ignore other factors such as weight, hair color, and so forth.

We could line up some drawn figures in size place too, by paying attention only to their height, as in Fig. 1.

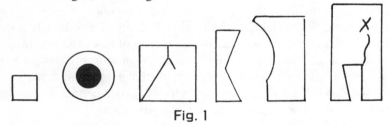

Fig. 1

We are then using a sequence rule of increasing amounts. (If we put the tallest figure first, we would have a sequence rule of *decreasing* amounts.)

We could also line figures up according to some other feature, instead of height.

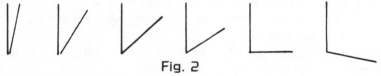

Fig. 2

In Fig. 2 they are lined up according to the size of the angle between the two lines.

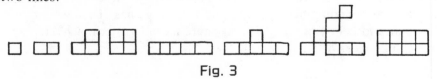

Fig. 3

In Fig. 3 they are lined up according to the area of each.

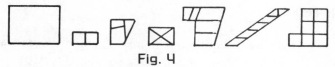

Fig. 4

In Fig. 4 they are lined up according to the number of regions in each.

Rules of Repetition.

You can also line up objects according to a rule of repetition, instead of a constantly increasing or decreasing amount of something. Fig. 5 shows a rule in which a mosaic tile inside a 2x2 grid rotates clockwise from tile to tile, repeating its position every four tiles. We say this rule has a *cycle* of four figures.

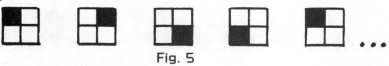

Fig. 5

Fig. 6 shows a rule in which the sequence *square, circle, triangle,* occurs over and over again. Here the rule has a cycle of three figures.

Fig. 6

Fig. 7 shows a sequence rule of *two white circles, then one black circle, repeat.* This rule, too, has a cycle of three.

Fig. 7

Two Factors

Suppose we take a simple cycle of two figures: *square, circle; repeat,* as in Fig. 8.

Fig. 8

We superimpose another cycle of three figures: *white, white, black; repeat.* Together we get the sequence shown in Fig. 9.

Fig. 9

Three Factors

We could also have a sequence with *three* factors: We start with a simple *color* rule with cycle of two: *white, black; repeat* (Fig. 10).

Fig. 10

We add a *size* rule with a cycle of three: *small, small, large; repeat* (Fig.11).

Fig. 11

Next we add a *shape* rule with a cycle of three: *circle, triangle, circle; repeat.*

We get a sequence with *three* rules. Fig. 12 shows it in the form of an intelligence test question.

Fig. 12

Finding the Rules with Two and Three Factor Sequences

An intelligence test may give you a sequence of figures and require you to find the rule. Usually you are asked to show you know the rule by telling what figure comes next.

To solve this kind of problem, notice *all* the ways the figures differ from each other. Among the most common ways are *shape, size, number, color,* and *position* (for example, *rotation*). Look for a *separate* rule for each way in which the figures are different. Look at Fig. 13.

Fig. 13

The figures differ in three features:
— *shape* (square, circle, triangle),
— *size* (small, large), and
— *color* (white, black, striped).

Let's find the rule for each feature separately.

Shape: We have square, circle, triangle / square, circle, triangle / square, circle, ?. There is a cycle of three. A *triangle* comes next.

Size: We have small, large / small, large / small, large / small, large / ? There is a cycle of two. *Small* comes next.

Color: We have white, striped, black, striped / white, striped, black, striped / ? There is a cycle of four. *White* comes next.

A *small, white triangle* comes next.

Sequence Problems

Draw the next figure in each of the following sequences. Check your answers in the back.

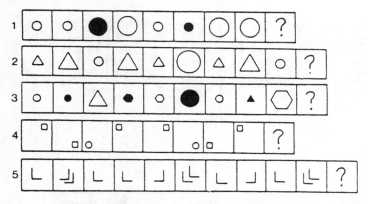

Sequence Games

Here are some games to give you practice in discovering sequence rules. In the first game, one player places mosaic pieces face down on a grid according to a sequence rule, and the other player(s) must discover the rule by turning the pieces face up one at a time.

*IND 1.

Aim of the Game: To find the rule for the sequence of mosaic tiles on a grid through uncovering.

Number of Players: Two or more.

Materials Needed: 4x4 grid; mosaic pieces.

How to Play: Player A

— decides on a sequence rule with a cycle no longer than four. The rule must involve a sequence laid down in one of the orders shown in Fig. 14.

— secretly fills up the entire grid with mosaic pieces according to the rule, starting in the upper left.

— turns all 16 mosaic pieces face down.

Fig. 15 shows a possible result of using each of these orders.

Player B chooses any mosaic piece to turn face up, then makes a guess as to the rule.

— If it is stated correctly, the game ends.

— If not, (with two players) Player B chooses another piece to turn face up; (with more than two players) The player's turn ends, the next player chooses a mosaic piece to turn face up, and the game continues as before.

If a player's guess accurately describes the mosaic pieces in the entire grid, it must be accepted as correct.

Player A gets one point for each tile the other players turn up. When a game ends, another player becomes Player A. Play continues until each player has had the same number of turns in each role. Player with most points wins.

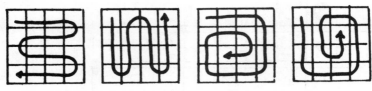

Fig. 14

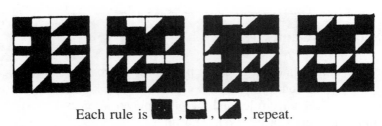

Each rule is ■ , ▣ , ◪ , repeat.

Fig. 15

In the last game, the other players uncover mosaic pieces to get information to discover the rule. In the next game the players suggest possible mosaic pieces in particular positions, and the rule-maker states whether they belong there or not.

* IND 2.

Aim of the Game: To find the rule for the sequence of mosaic pieces on the grid through placing pieces.

Number of Players: Two or more.

Materials Needed: 8x8 grid; mosaic pieces.
How to Play: Player A
— decides on a sequence rule with a cycle no longer than four. The rule must involve a sequence laid down in one of the orders shown in Fig. 14.
— secretly fills up the entire grid with mosaic pieces according to the rule, starting in the upper left.
— turns all 16 mosaic pieces face down.
Fig. 15 shows a possible result of using each of these orders.

Player B chooses any mosaic piece to place in any position and orientation face up on the grid.
— If the rule allows it to be placed there, the rule-maker says so.
If not, the rule-maker removes it.
Player B then makes a guess as to the rule.
— If it is stated correctly, the game ends.
— If not, (with two players) Player B chooses another piece to place on the grid; (with more than two players) the player's turn ends, the next player chooses a mosaic piece to place on the grid and the game continues as before.

If a player's guess accurately describes the mosaic pieces in the entire grid, it must be accepted as correct.

Player A gets one point for each tile the other players turn up. When a game ends, another player becomes Player A. Play continues until each player has had the same number of turns in each role. Player with most points wins.

Note that this game requires you to remember which mosaic pieces have not been allowed on which grid squares.

Discovering Mosaic Pattern Rules

We have seen that the grid can be used to play games of discovering sequence rules and matrix rules. It can also be used to play games of discovering the rules for mosaic patterns (which you became familiar with in the MOSAICS chapter). In the next game, one player arranges mosaic pieces in a pattern face down on a grid, and the other player(s) must discover the pattern by turning the pieces up one at a time.

*IND 3.
Aim of the Game: To find the mosaic pattern in the grid through uncovering.
Number of Players: Two or more.
Materials Needed: 4x4 grid; mosaic pieces.

How to Play: Player A
— secretly fills up the entire grid with a pattern that is symmetric in at least *one* of these ways: horizontally, vertically, diagonally, as in Fig. 16. (See Chapter II if you don't remember what this means.)
— turns all 16 mosaic pieces face down.
    Player B chooses any mosaic piece to turn face up, then makes a guess as to the pattern.
— If it is described correctly, the game ends.
— If not, (with two players) Player B chooses another piece to turn face up;(with more than two players) The player's turn ends,the next player chooses a mosaic piece to turn face up, and the game continues as before.
    If a player's guess accurately describes the pattern, it must be accepted as correct.
    Player A gets one point for each tile the other players turn up. When a game ends, another player becomes Player A. Play continues until each player has had the same number of turns in each role. Player with most points wins.
    In the next game, one player arranges mosaic pieces in a pattern face down on a grid, and the other player(s) must discover the pattern by placing pieces on the grid one at a time.

*IND 4.
Aim of the Game: To find the mosaic pattern in the grid through placing pieces.
Number of Players: Two or more.
Materials Needed: 8x8 grid; mosaic pieces.
How to Play: Player A
— secretly fills up the entire grid with a pattern that is symmetric in at least *one* of these ways: horizontally, vertically, diagonally.
— turns all 16 mosaic pieces face down.
    Player B chooses any mosaic piece to place in any position and orientation face up on the grid.
— If the pattern allows it to be placed there, the rule-maker says so.
— If not, the rule-maker removes it.
    Player B then makes a guess as to the pattern.
— If it is described correctly, the game ends.
— If not, (with two players) Player B chooses another piece to place on the grid; (with more than two players). The player's turn ends, the next player chooses a mosaic piece to place on the grid and the game continues as before.
    If a player's guess accurately describes the pattern, it must be accepted as correct.

Player A gets one point for each tile the other players turn up. When a game ends, another player becomes Player A. Play continues until each player has had the same number of turns in each role. Player with most points wins.

Note that this game requires you to remember which mosaic pieces have not been allowed on which grid squares.

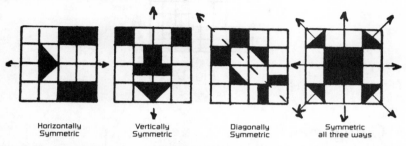

| Horizontally Symmetric | Vertically Symmetric | Diagonally Symmetric | Symmetric all three ways |

Fig. 16

Discovering Photographic Subjects from Pieces

We have seen how the grid can be used to discover
— sequence rules
— matrix rules
— rules for mosaic patterns.

In each case you use *inductive logic*, putting together pieces of information to reach a general conclusion about abstract figures, such as circles, triangles, and mosaic pieces. Next we will give you practice reaching a conclusion about more meaningful "figures" from everyday life.

In the following game, a newspaper photograph is covered with mosaic pieces. The players must discover the subject of the photograph by uncovering pieces one at a time.

*IND 5.

Aim of the Game: To discover what photograph is hidden by the mosaic tiles.

Number of Players: Two.

Materials Needed: Newspaper or magazine photographs, mosaic tiles.

How to Play: Player A cuts out a newspaper or magazine picture of something that can be easily and clearly described: a well-known person, a plane crash, a football catch, etc., and covers it completely with mosaic tiles. Player B removes the tiles one by one (Fig. 17). After each tile is removed, Player B guesses the general theme of what is in the photo (not the details). The game ends when Player B guesses correctly.

Play continues until each player has had the same number of turns in each role. Player A gets one point for each tile Player B removes. Player with most points wins.

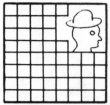

Fig. 17

Categories

We have been focusing so far on rules that relate one element, such as a circle, triangle, or mosaic piece, to the ones around it: to the left, right, above and below. Another basic kind of rule lets you place elements into categories. This kind of rule tells what belongs in a category, and what does not.

Suppose you were told that your grandfather, your third-grade teacher, the President of the United States, and the waiter in your favorite restaurant belong in a category, and your car, the Empire State Building, tomatoes, and rain do not belong in that category, You could make up two lists:

BELONGS IN CATEGORY	DOESN'T BELONG IN CATEGORY
My grandfather	My car
My third-grade teacher	The Empire State Building
The President of the U.S.	Tomatoes
The waiter in my favorite restaurant	Rain

and easily figure out that the rule is *people* belong, *nonpeople* do not.

Here's a game about discovering the rules for categories in which all the things that belong are simple drawings.

*IND 6.

Aim of the Game: To discover which drawings belong in the category.

Number of Players: Two.

Materials Needed: Paper, pencils.

How to Play:

a.   Player A secretly writes down the rule for what drawings belong to the category. The rule may deal only with *one* feature of the drawings, for example, curved vs. straight lines, or white vs. shaded figures.

b.   Player A then draws and shows to Player B one object that belongs in the category, and one object that does not, using the format shown in Fig. 18.

c.   Player B then draws a new object on his/her own paper.

d.   Player A states whether B's drawing is in the category.
— If it is, A redraws it in the "YES" row.
— If it isn't, A redraws it in the "NO" row.

e.   Player B then has a chance to state the rule.
— If B is correct, the game ends, and the players switch roles and play again.
— If not, B draws another object, and Player A continues as before.

The game continues until Player B correctly states the rule. Player A gets one point for each object Player B draws. Play continues until each player has had the same number of turns as rule-maker. Player with most points wins.

Variation: The rule deals with two factors at once. For example, drawings in the category must be shaded, and made up of straight lines (Fig. 19).

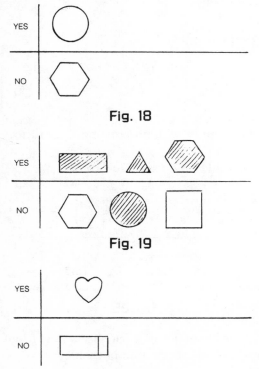

Fig. 18

Fig. 19

Fig. 20

Among the factors you can use in this game are: curved vs. straight lines; regular vs. irregular polygons; shaded vs. solid figures; open vs. closed figures; symmetrical vs. nonsymmetrical figures; simple vs. complex figures, etc.

Here's how a sample game might go.

Player A's sheet at first looks like Fig. 20.

B: Does this fit? (Fig. 21).

A: Yes.

B: The rule is figures made only of curved lines fit.

A: No, that's not the rule.

Fig. 21

B: Does this fit? (Fig. 22)

A: Yes.

B: Every figure fits unless it's made up only of straight lines.

A: No, that's not it.

Fig. 22

B: Does this fit? (Fig. 23)

A: No.

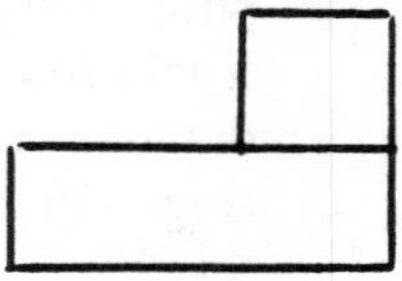

B: Figures with all right angles do not fit.

A: No, that isn't the rule.

Fig. 23

B: Does this fit? (Fig. 24)

A: Yes.

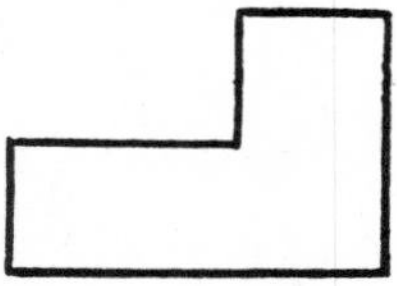

Fig. 24

B: The rule is that figures with no crossing lines fit the category.

A: Yes!

Player A's sheet would now look like Fig. 25.

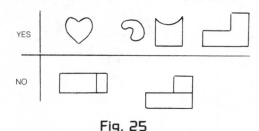

YES

NO

Fig. 25

Fig. 26 shows some examples of what sheets might look like at the end of several games. Can you tell the rule in each case?

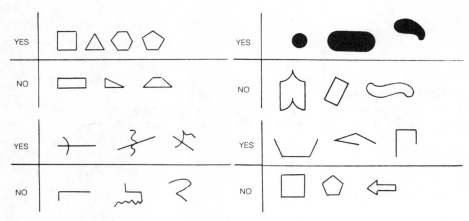

Fig. 26

Here is a summary of the general principles you can learn from the games and puzzles in this chapter:

— Try simple rules first.

— List possibilities, get more information, then eliminate possibilities.

— Pay attention to all changes from one event to a "similar" event.

— See what things that *don't* fit a rule have in common.

— Look for a *cycle,* which is a complete set of changes before a pattern repeats.

Solutions

Page 127

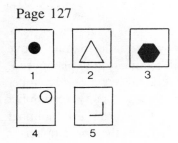

Page 135

1. Yes = regular polygon
2. Yes = crossed lines
3. Yes = black, curved
4. Yes = open figure

CHAPTER XII

VISUAL STRATEGY

Strategy deals with making plans to reach your goals. If your goal is to travel from one city to another, at the first stage of planning you may decide whether to take a plane, a train, a bus, walk, or hitchhike. After you make a plan, you usually have some additional choices to make. If you decide to fly, you then decide which airline to take, when to leave, how to get to the airport, etc. The choices you have for carrying out a plan are called *tactics*. If your strategy for getting from one city to another is to hitchhike, your *tactics* might include carrying an easy-to-read sign that gives your destination, waiting at a point on the road when cars are forced to go slowly and have the opportunity to stop, etc.

Being Last

In the first section of games of visual strategy, your goal is to draw, move or place the last object. As you will see, this will require you to plan ahead. Try to arrange things so that on your move there is always an *odd* number of moves left, and on your opponent's turn there are always an *even* number of moves left. Then eventually your opponent will have the *even* number of *two* moves left, and make one of them, leaving you the *odd* number of *one* move left. When you make it, you have made the last move and won.

In this first game players alternately extend a line on a grid of dots without forming a loop.

*STR 1.
Aim of the Game: To avoid forming a closed loop.
Number of Players: Two.
Materials Needed: Pencil and paper; a 3x3 grid of dots on graph paper.

How to Play: Player A draws a horizontal or vertical line from any dot to an adjacent one. Players B and A then alternate turns. On each turn, a player begins where the line ended on the last turn, and extends the line horizontally or vertically to an adjacent dot. Game continues until one player's line closes a loop, as in Fig. 1, diagram 8. The other player wins.

Variation: Start with a 4x5 or 5x6 grid.

Variation: Start with a 4x5 grid; aim is to close a loop instead of to avoid closing a loop.

Variation: Start with a 4x5 grid. You can extend the line from either end.

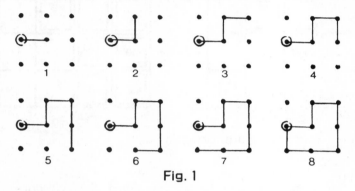

Fig. 1

Play this game a few times to get familiar with it. Notice that there are only three different beginning moves: from the center, from a corner, or from the middle of an edge. If you go first and start from the center or a corner, the other player can force a win. If you begin from the middle of an edge, you can force a win (Fig. 1).

In the previous game you had to extend the end of a line. In the next game you have more options for your move.

*STR 2.

Aim of the Game: To place the last mosaic piece on a 4x4 grid.

Number of Players: Two.

Materials Needed: Paper and pencil.

Preparation: Draw a 4x4 grid.

How to Play: Players alternate placing mosaic pieces in an empty square of the grid. Each mosaic piece must be placed in the same *row* or *column* as the last one. Each piece must be placed either adjacent to the last one, or separated from it only by empty squares.

Fig. 2a shows the beginning of a sample game, in which the numbers "1" and "2" show the order of play. The "3" can be placed

— in square A or B, the same column as "2," the last square placed, and adjacent to it.

— in square C, the same row as "2," and separated only by an empty square (B).

— in square D, the same row as "2," and adjacent to it.

But the "3" cannot be placed in square E, which is in the same row as "2" but separated from it by a filled square.

Fig. 2b shows a different completed sample game.

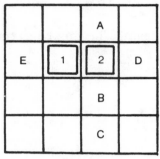

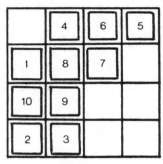

Fig. 2a   Fig. 2b

Variations: Start with 5x5 or 6x6 grid.

*STR 3.

Aim of the Game: To draw the last line connecting two dots or one dot with itself.

Number of Players: Two.

Materials Needed: Paper and pencil.

Preparation: Three dots are randomly placed on the paper, with lots of space between them.

How to Play: Each player in turn

— draws a smooth curved line from one dot to another or back to itself.

— Then adds a new dot anywhere along the connecting line.

   There are two restrictions:

— A line may not cross itself or any other line.

— No dot may have more than three lines coming out of it.

   Game continues until one player cannot draw a new line according to the rules. The other player wins.

Variations: Start with 4, 5, 8 or 10 dots.

   Fig. 3 shows a sample game.

*STR 4.

Aim of the Game: To draw the last right triangle on the grid.

Number of Players: Two.

Materials Needed: Grid of dots 4x4 on graph paper.

How to Play: Each player in turn draws a right triangle by connecting three dots. The short sides of the triangle must be horizontal and vertical, and the triangle must cover one half of a grid square. No triangle may touch any other triangle, even at a point. The player who places the last triangle wins.

Variation: Use 5x5 grid.

Variation: Each short side may connect two or three dots horizontally or vertically (Fig. 4).

Here are two sample games (Fig. 5a, 5b). The numbers show the order in which the triangles were drawn.

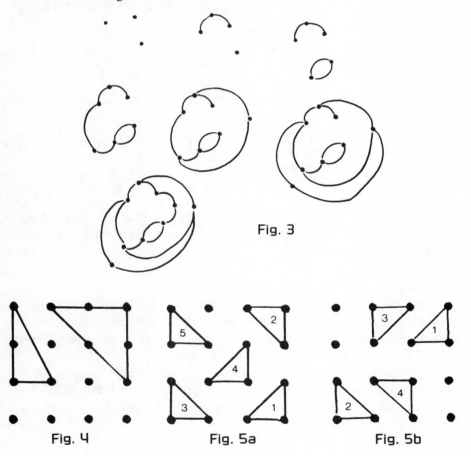

Fig. 3

Fig. 4   Fig. 5a   Fig. 5b

In the next set of games, both players place figures anywhere inside a square boundary, each trying to place the last figure.

*STR 5.

Aim of the Game: To place the last piece inside the boundaries of a square.

Number of Players: Two.

Materials Needed: 4x4 grid; monomino pieces.

How to Play: Players alternately place monomino pieces on the grid. No monomino piece may touch any other, even at a point. The player who places the last piece wins (Fig. 6).

Variation: Use domino pieces instead of monomino pieces.

Variation: Use tetraminoes instead of monomino pieces.

Variation: Use pentomino pieces instead of monomino pieces.

Variation: Each player chooses a different pentomino piece as a model. On each turn the player traces his/her model anywhere within the boundaries of the grid. Players then switch pieces with each other and repeat game.

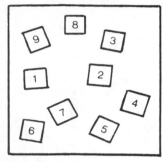

Fig. 6

Try each of these variations to increase your skill in this game. Invent your own variations. For example, on each turn a player may place either a monomino piece or a domino.

Being First

In all the games so far in this chapter you have tried to be the *last* to do something, connect dots, extend a line, and so on. In the next group of games, you try to be the *first* to do something.

For convenience, we will refer to "black" and "white" mosaic pieces; you may use any two different kinds of mosaic pieces, such as ■ and ◪.

In the next game you try to be first to get rid of your pieces by moving them off the grid.

*STR 6.

Aim of the Game: To be first to move your pieces off the grid.

Number of Players: Two.

Materials Needed: 4x4 grid; three black and three white monomino pieces.

How to Play: The pieces are first arranged on the grid as shown in Fig. 7.

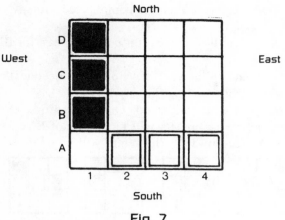

Fig. 7

Players alternate moves, on each turn moving one piece to an adjacent empty square. White can only move north, east or west; Black can only move east, north or south. A white piece in row D can move (north) off the grid; and a black piece in column 4 can move (east) off the grid. Each player must always leave the other player a legal move. The first player to get both pieces off the board wins.

Variation: Use 3x3 grid; two black and two white pieces; start with southwest corner empty.

Variation: Use 5x5 grid; four black and four white pieces; start with southwest corner empty.

Suppose in the variation with the 3x3 grid, both players use the following simple strategy with just one rule of action:

— go forward directly to the goal (north for White, east for Black) on each move if possible.

Fig. 8 shows how a game might go. White may start as in Fig. 8a. By Fig. 8h you can see that White will lose; White needs three more moves to win, Black only needs two. White loses even though White went first.

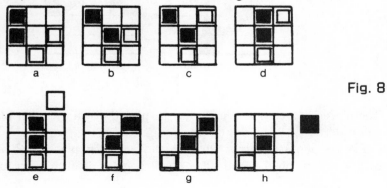

Fig. 8

Suppose now both players use a more complicated strategy with *two* rules of action:
— go forward directly to the goal (north for White, east for Black) on each move if possible.
— if there is a choice of moves forward, pick the one that blocks an opponent's piece from moving directly forward.

Fig. 9 shows how a game might go. On White's first move there is a choice: the move shown in Fig. 9a will block one of Black's pieces from moving forward. As seen by Fig. 9h, White will win.

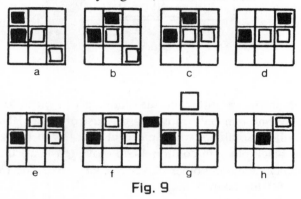

Fig. 9

*STR 7.
Aim of the Game: To complete a solid black path from one side of the grid to an opposite side.
Number of Players: Two.
Materials Needed: 5x5 grid; mosaic tiles.
How to Play: Player A tries to form a solid black path from left to right side, Player B from top to bottom (Fig. 10).

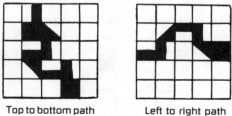

Top to bottom path   Left to right path

Fig. 10

The pieces in a complete path may be placed down by either player and in any order.

Players alternate turns. On each turn a player places one piece in any empty square on the grid. The black portion of each piece placed must connect with the black portion of the other pieces it shares a side with (See Fig. 11).

Fig. 11

Variation: Use 6x6 or 8x8 grid.

A good strategy here is to space out your pieces and connect them only when necessary in response to your opponent's actions. Do not try to create a path piece by piece, for example, in Fig. 12 it would be better to place a ■ in square B3 than in B2 or B4.

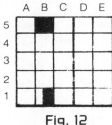

Fig. 12

*STR 8.

Aim of the Game: To be first to get three mosaic pieces in a row horizontally, vertically or diagonally by placing or moving them.

Number of Players: Two.

Materials Needed: Three ■ and three ◩ mosaic pieces; 3x3 grid.

How to Play: Each player uses one kind of mosaic piece. Players alternate turns.

In the first phase, on each turn a player places one mosaic piece on an empty square of the grid. Exception: the first player is not allowed to place a piece on the center square (B2 in Fig. 13) of the grid.

If there is no winner when all six pieces are placed, the game enters the second phase. Players continue to alternate turns; on each turn, a player moves one card horizontally, vertically or diagonally to an empty adjacent square.

The game ends when one player gets three mosaic pieces in a row, or when both players agree to a draw.

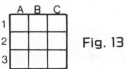

Fig. 13

In the next group of games, your goal is to be first to create some particular kind of formation. In the first case, to get four of your mosaic pieces in a row on a grid.

*STR 9.

Aim of the Game: To be first to get four of your mosaic pieces in a row horizontally, vertically or diagonally.
Number of Players: Two.
Materials Needed: Grid 8x8, solid mosaic pieces of black and white.
How to Play: Players alternate turns, one with black pieces, other with white. First player places a piece on any grid square. On each subsequent turn, the player places a piece on a empty square of the grid, touching the side or corner of at least one other piece. The first to arrange four pieces in a horizontal, vertical or diagonal row wins.

Fig. 14 shows the beginning of a sample game. The numbers inside the mosaic pieces show the order in which they were placed down.

1. D4   White begins by placing a piece into a central position that allows a possible four in a row in eight different directions.
2. E4   Black responds by placing a piece into another central position. This piece cramps White's expansion to the right along row 4, but at the same time it limits Black's expansion to the left along row 4.
3. E3   White threatens to make a diagonal row.
4. C5   Black breaks up the threat at one end.
5. C3   White threatens to get three-in-a-row, open at both ends, in several places at once, by making the next move at B2, E5, or D3. Black cannot meet all these threats at once, and will lose.

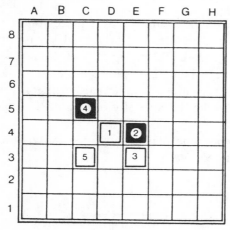

Fig. 14

In the next case, your goal is to get four of your mosaic pieces in consecutive locations on an actual map.

*STR 10.
Aim of the Game: To line up four tokens of the same color on four consecutive intersections of the routes of a map.
Number of Players: Two.
Materials Needed: Automobile map that clearly shows major highways; six blue and six red tokens.
Preparation: Players decide which they will consider the major highways (let us say here, for example, all those represented by thick red lines).
How to Play: Players alternate turns, one using the red tokens, the other, the blue. On each turn a player either
— places a token from his/her hand at a route intersection of the map, or
— moves a token already on the map to an adjacent intersection.

Tokens may only be placed on the map where three or more thick red lines converge. A token may not be placed on top of another. Each player attempts to line up four tokens in consecutive intersections. In Fig. 15, a move from "D" to "E" will produce a win with four consecutive intersections covered by tokens of the same color.

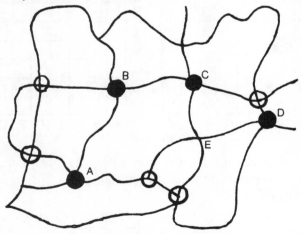

Fig. 15

*STR 11.
Aim of the Game: To locate and sink your opponent's ships.
Number of Players: Two.
Materials Needed: Four 10x10 grids, two pencils.
Preparation: Each player secretly records on one grid the location of one battleship (a horizontal or vertical line of four adjacent squares), two cruisers

(each a horizontal or vertical line of three adjacent squares), and three destroyers (each consisting of two horizontally or vertically adjacent squares), and four submarines (one square each), as in Fig. 16. Each player uses a second grid to record progress in locating the opponent's ships.

How to Play: Players alternate turns.

a.   On each turn a player "fires a shot" by calling out the locations of two horizontally or vertically connected squares (for example, "E7 and E8!").

b.   The other player then calls out wether the shot was
      — a "hit" (a ship is on one or both of these squares), or
      — a "miss" (no ship on either square).

c.   Both players record the results of the shot.

d.   The other player fires a shot.

   The game continues until every square of each ship of one of the players has been hit. That player loses.

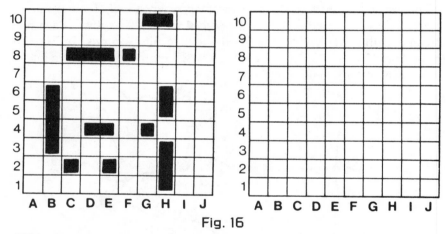

Fig. 16

   With the set-up in Fig. 16, the following sequence of the opponent's shots, results, and reasoning could occur:

-E7,E8   Hit (Fig. 17).

Fig. 17

-D7,E7   Miss (Fig. 18).

Player knows now that E8 contains part of a ship, which does not extend downward to E7.

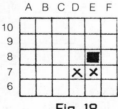

Fig. 18

-E9,E10   Miss (Fig. 19).

Player knows ship doesn't extend upward to E9.

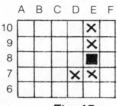

Fig. 19

-C8,D8   Hit (Fig. 20).

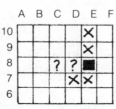

Fig. 20

This last hit might mean a ship in C8 (Fig. 21a), a ship in D8 (Fig. 21b), or ships in both C8 and D8 (Fig. 21c).

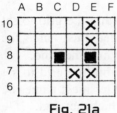
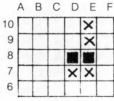
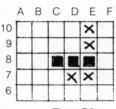

Fig. 21a   **Fig. 21b**   **Fig. 21c**

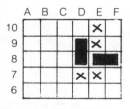

Fig. 22

Keep in mind that if you find both D8 and E8 contain part of a ship, they may be parts of *different* ships, as in Fig. 22!

*STR 12.

Aim of the Game: To find the boundary between the two areas of the grid by asking the fewest questions.

Number of Players: Two.

Materials Needed: Two 8x8 grids of squares on graph paper; two pencils; ruler.

How to Play: One player is area-builder, the other is area-finder. On one grid the area-builder secretly chooses one square inside the grid, and draws two straight lines from a point within this square to two squares on the edge of the grid, completely dividing the grid into two areas, P and Q (Fig. 23a).

a.   Area-finder names a grid square (for example, C7).

b.   Area-builder tells whether it is
      — in P,
      — in Q, or
      — partly in P and partly in Q.

c.   Area-finder records the result on his/her own grid.

d.   Area-finder may make a guess as to the square from which, and the two squares to which, the two lines were drawn.

e.   Area-finder continues to ask about other grid squares until s/he correctly identifies the boundary between areas P and Q by naming the square from which the lines start, and the two squares in which they end.

f.   Then the two players switch roles. The player who locates the boundary line with fewer questions wins.

Variation: Draw three straight lines from the square within the grid to set up three areas, P, Q and R (Fig. 23b). The area-builder must name the square from which the lines start, and the three squares in which they end.

Variation: Draw four straight lines from the square within the grid to set up four areas, P, Q, R and S (Fig. 23c). The area-builder must name the square from which the lines start, and the four squares in which they end.

Variation: Use a 10 x 10 or 12 x 12 grid.

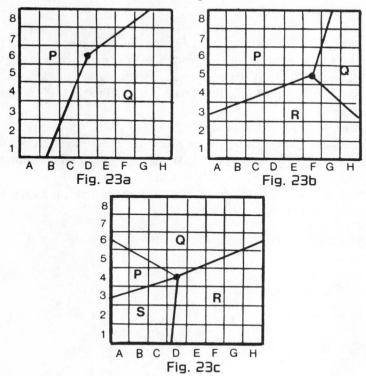

Fig. 23a   Fig. 23b

Fig. 23c

General Strategic Principles

From the many stategy games in this chapter, some general strategic principles emerge that one can apply in new situations beyond the games:

1. Plan how to reach your objectives.

   In STR 1, if you begin from the middle of an edge, you can force a win.

2. Anticipate your opponent's moves.

3. Record your moves so you can learn from your experiences.

   In STR 4, by numbering the triangles you can reconnstruct the game.

4. "Different" patterns may actually be the same.

   In STR 1, there are only three different beginning moves.

5. Develop rules that eliminate possibilities.

6. Set up subgoals.

7. Work backwards from the goal.

8. Watch your opponent's moves.

   In STR 6, if there is a choice of moves forward, you pick the one that blocks an opponent's piece from moving directly forward.

9. Carry out a diversionary attack; then attack elsewhere. (Disguise your plans).
10. Prepare your development; don't aim directly at the goal.
   In STR 7, a good strategy is to space out your pieces and connect them only when necessary in response to your opponent's actions.
11. Make sure there is not an immeadiate threat to your losing.
   In the sample game of STR 9, Black's second move (to C5) counters a threat.
12. Look for all possibilities.
13. Recognize patterns; know what to do with a pattern you recognize.
   In the sample game of STR 9, White recognizes an opportunity to move to C3 and make several threats at once.
14. You can obtain strategic principles through logic, others' experience, and your own experiencce.

CHAPTER XIII

MEMORY

In this chapter we teach you how to improve your memory for visual shapes, how to associate shapes with other shapes and with words, and how to use visualization to link words with each other. We will present some general principles of memory improvement, and relate them specifically to visual materials. We will also provide games and other activities to give you practice in learning these principles and applying them to everyday situations. To begin with, though, let's consider how well you can remember *verbal* material.

Remembering Words and Visual Material

Remembering a List of Words

How easily can you memorize a list of words? It depends, you will say, on how many words and what words they are. Here are five lists, each 12 items long. The items in the first list are made-up words; in each of the other lists, they are real words.

List 1	List 2	List 3	List 4	List 5
W	crayak	refrigerator	motor	Johnny
D	flabon	magazine	hood	is
Q	remler	chair	axle	going
L	jassel	pencil	tire	into
C	whickle	lawyer	gas	the
Y	tresol	bus	fender	city
F	birtop	wallet	radiator	to
H	menult	horse	brake	buy
B	ponthal	television	clutch	a
J	scarage	barn	bumper	container
R	zakler	hamburger	plugs	of
N	urko	tree	distributor	milk

Study the first list for a minute. Then immediately write down as many of the items as you remember. Do the same with each of the other four lists.

1. If you are like most people, you will find the first list very hard to remember. We are used to seeing letters grouped into words. But the letters in List 1 have no special meaning to us. It's hard to remember which letters were on the list, and which weren't.
2. You'll also find List 2 quite difficult. Here the letters are grouped into words, but the words are not at all familiar. In fact they are imaginary words.
3. List 3 is easier. Each item is a familiar word.
4. List 4 also contains familiar words, and each one is related to automobiles. If you know something about automobiles, you may have found List 4 easier than List 3.
5. List 5 contains familiar words arranged in a sentence. You are likely to remember all 12 items, *and* the order in which you read them.

   If you had been given the list in the order *container, is, buy, the, Johnny, city, milk, into, of, to, going, a,* you would have had more trouble.

You see that how easily you can remember a list of 12 verbal items depends on

— how meaningful the items are to you,
— how familiar you are with them, and
— how the items are related to each other.

Remembering Visual Material

The same is true in remembering visual material. How easily do you think you could memorize the exact positions of 64 mosaic pieces arranged in a 8x8 square?

Look at Figs. 1a, 1b, 1c and 1d.

Fig. 1a

Fig. 1b

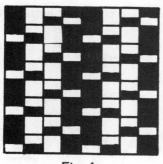

Fig. 1c

Fig. 1d

1.   The mosaic pieces in Fig. 1a have been placed down at random. You will find it quite difficult to remember this arrangement.

2.   The pieces in Fig. 1b are arranged into an intricate design; with some effort, you could remember it.

3.   The pieces in Fig. 1c have been arranged in a repeated sequence, snaking around from left to right. You could easily remember this arrangement, and reproduce it even a week later.

4.   The pieces in Fig. 1d have been placed to form a meaningful figure; it would be easy to remember what the figure is, and with a little effort, to remember its size, position on the grid, and how it was formed. You could remember it, too, even a week later.

You see that meaning, familiarity, and relations among the items can make it easier to memorize visual material, just as these factors make it easier to memorize verbal material. In this chapter we will show you how to make a hard memory task easier, by using systems based upon principles of meaningfulness, familiarity, organization and association.

Systems for Linking Words and Pictures

Certain methods called mnemonics can help us improve our memories. The most basic principle is to associate one thing with another, new things with old. We can improve our memory by always practicing making associations, first in small matters, and as we get better at it and enjoy our success in it, in larger, more complicated tasks. In general we learn and remember more easily

— when the material to be learned is organized.

— when the material is meaningful.

— when the material is related to things we already know.

— when we actively try to associate words to pictures, and new things to things we already know.

Applying the Visualization Method in Remembering Shapes

Suppose you wanted to remember the shapes shown in Fig. 2 well enough to rapidly sketch out all 12.

Here's a two-stage strategy you could use:

1.   Find a word that you can easily associate with each shape (for example, see Fig. 3).

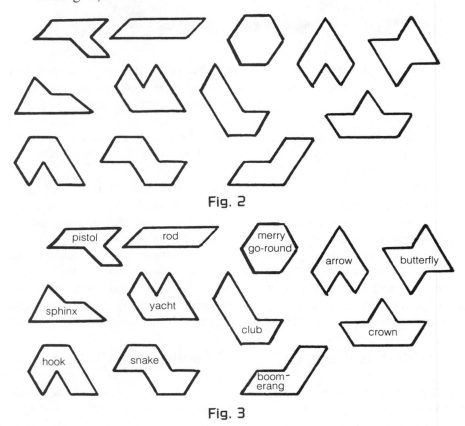

Fig. 2

Fig. 3

2.   Develop a set of action pictures that link these words into a chain of pairs, the first with the second, the second with the third, etc. For example, the *snake* is wrapped around the *sphinx*, the *sphinx* is hit by the *arrow*, etc.

Now, when you want to quickly sketch out all 12 shapes, remember the first picture in your mind, the *snake* is wrapped around the *sphinx*, draw the snake and sphinx shapes, then remember the second picture, etc.

Memory Games

Here is a game in which you can apply the visualization method of linking pairs of objects in a series of pictures to remember a list.

*MEM 1.
Aim of the Game: To notice what object is missing from a display.
Number of Players: Two or more.
Materials Needed: A dozen objects from the players' pockets.
How to Play: Players take 12 objects from their pockets (key, change, credit card, pocket knife, driver's license, etc.) and place them on the table. One player leaves the room. Remaining players remove one object from the table and place it out of view. The returning player must state what was removed.

To succeed in this game, link the objects in mental pictures, two at a time, just as you did with the hexiamonds. After an object is removed, you can run through your chain of pictures to see what is missing.

Now here's a game where you can use the principle of "organization."

*MEM 2.
Aim of the Game: To reproduce exactly a 4x4 mosaic.
Number of Players: Two.
Materials Needed: Mosaic tiles.
How to Play: Player A constructs a 4x4 mosaic that is horizontally and vertically symmetric (Fig. 4a). Player B studies it for 30 seconds, then Player A covers it. Player B must now build an exact copy of the mosaic. If correct, Player B gets one point; if not, Player A gets one point. Then players switch roles. After an equal number of turns in each role, the player with more points wins.
Variation: Use a 6x6 mosaic (Fig. 4c), instead of a 4x4.

To succeed in this game, take advantage of the organization of the material to be learned. Remember the list of words above was easier to learn when the words were organized into a sentence, and the mosaics above were easier to remember when organized into a repeated pattern or organized to form a picture.

In this situation, the *horizontal and vertical symmetry* gives organization to the entire 4x4 mosaic. Memorize only the 2x2 mosaic in the upper left (Fig. 4b) and you will be able to reproduce the entire 4x4 mosaic. When you play the **Variation** to *MEM 2, memorize only the 3x3 mosaic in the upper left (Fig. 4d) and you will be able to reproduce the entire 6x6 mosaic.

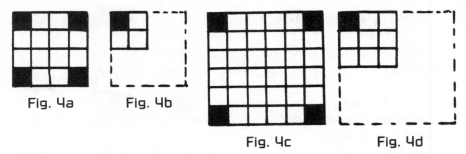

Fig. 4a   Fig. 4b

Fig. 4c   Fig. 4d

*MEM 3.

Aim of the Game: To reproduce five connected lines drawn on a grid.
Number of Players: Two.
Materials Needed: Grid of boxes 6x6 on graph paper.
How to Play: Player A draws a heavy line, with no more than four bends in it, along the grid lines. The line may bend only where grid lines intersect (Fig. 5). Player B studies it for 30 seconds, then Player A covers it. Player B must now build an exact copy of the line. If correct, Player B gets one point. Then players switch roles. After an equal number of turns in each role, the player with more points wins.
Variation: Use a 8x8 grid, instead of 6x6.
Variation: Use a line that bends no more than seven times, instead of four.

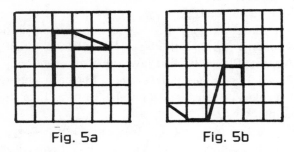

Fig. 5a   Fig. 5b

In this game, as Player B, try to associate an object with the line drawn. For example, you might see Fig. 5a as the head and neck of an animal, and Fig. 5b as a person praying. As Player A, try to make the line as "abstract" as possible.

See what mnemonic methods you can come up with to do well in the next two games.

*MEM 4.

Aim of the Game: To find out which tile in the mosaic has been rotated.
Number of Players: Two.
Materials Needed: 4x4 grid; mosaic tiles.

How to Play: Player A constructs a 4x4 mosaic which Player B studies for 30 seconds. Then, with Player B not looking, Player A rotates one tile of the mosaic by 90 or 180 degrees (Fig 6). Player B must now turn back to its original position the tile he/she thinks has been rotated. If correct, Player B gets one point. Then players switch roles. After an equal number of turns in each role, the player with more points wins.

Variation: Player A rotates two tiles, instead of one. Player B gets one point for each tile returned to its original position.

Variation: Use 6x6 mosaic, instead of 4x4, and rotate two tiles, instead of one. Player B gets one point for each tile returned to its original position.

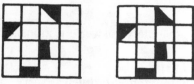

Fig. 6

As Player B, try to form an association with the original mosaic so that you will notice any change. As Player A, try to build the original mosaic so that it is as hard as possible to form an association to it.

*MEM 5.

Aim of the Game: To locate as many pairs as possible among face-down mosaic pieces.

Number of Players: Two or more.

Materials Needed: 20 mosaic pieces, four each of five different mosaic pieces.

How to Play: The mosaic pieces are dealt out at random face down in four rows of five each, as shown in Fig. 7.

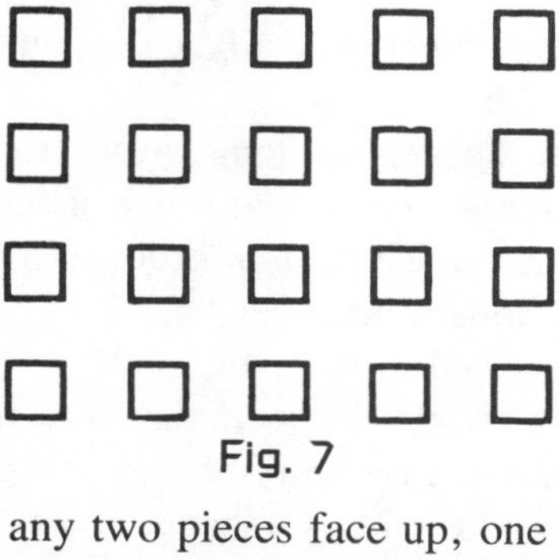

Fig. 7

The first player turns any two pieces face up, one at a time, searching for a pair. The other players can see the pieces when turned face-up. A player who turns up a pair puts them aside, and then takes another turn.

The orientation of a piece doesn't matter. ⬓ is considered the same as ◨. Together they are a pair. ◪ is considered the same as ◩, etc.

Otherwise the player turns them face down again in their original positions and orientations, and then the turn passes to the next player.

The game continues until all the pieces have been taken as pairs by the players. The winner is the player with the most mosaic pieces.

Variation: Use 30 mosaic pieces, six of each kind, dealt out in five rows of six each.

Play a "solitaire" version of this game by yourself to get familiar with it. See if you can develop your own approach to winning.

***MEM 6.**

Aim of the Game: To accurately answer questions about a picture you have briefly seen.

Number of Players: Two.

Materials Needed: Photographs from newspapers, books, or magazines.

How to Play: Player A chooses a photograph of a complex scene (a street scene, for example, not the portrait of one person), and shows it to Player B for 30 seconds. Player A then takes it away, and asks Player B three general questions about the photograph. For example,

— How many people were in the photograph?

— How many cars were in the photograph?

— Was there a restaurant in the photograph?

Player B gets one point for each question correctly answered. Then players switch roles, and a new photograph is chosen. After an equal number of turns in each role, the player with more points wins.

Variation: Ask more detailed questions. For example, Was the man on the left wearing a jacket?

*** MEM 7.**

Aim of the Game: To remember in detail the placing of objects in a box.

Number of Players: Two or more.

Materials Needed: Ten household items; a box to hold them.

How to Play: One player writes down a list of the objects, then, in view of the others, places each object in that order into the box, and covers the box. Each other player must remember:

1) what items were placed in the box.
2) the order in which they have been placed in the box.
3) the location of each item within the box (corner, side, etc.)
4) descriptive details of the items (shape, color, size, etc.)

Points are awarded in each of the four categories above, for each correct response beyond the first four items, as follows:

For (1), items placed, a player gets one point for each item (beyond four) correctly named.

For (2), order of placement, a player gets one point for each item (beyond four) in the exact order placed, minus two points for each item not in the exact order.

For (3), location, a player gets one point for each item (beyond four) correctly placed.

For (4), details, a player gets two points for each item (beyond four) correctly described.

Variation: Use more items for greater difficulty.

Applying Memory Systems in Everyday Life

Everyone wants to recognize people they have met before. That is one common area where you can apply your memory systems.

Try to link something you notice about someone's appearance to his or her name. Make the link *vivid*, no matter how far-fetched. For example, if Mr. Edward Booth always wears large round eyeglasses, you might form a mental image like that in Fig. 8.

Mr. B   TH

Fig. 8

There are also many other applications in school, work and everyday activities. In schoolwork, there are three different types of memory situations you may encounter:

1. You study some material, and you know exactly what you will be asked. For example, you memorize a list of presidents of the United States, or the capital cities of each state. You know you will be asked such questions as:
    — Who was the President after Abraham Lincoln?
    — What is the capital of the state of Arkansas?
    Games *MEM 1 through *MEM 5 prepare you for this type of situation. In these games you know what the *possible* questions are, but you may not know just which ones will be asked.
2. You study some material, but you don't know what kinds of questions will be asked. For example, after you study biographic material about the presidents, you may be asked such questions as:

— In what year was President Lincoln born?

— Which presidents of the United States served in the Army?

Game *MEM 6 helps prepare you for this kind of memory situation.

3.   You study some material, and can expect questions that go beyond the facts given, to force you to make an *interpretation* or show you *understand* the significance of something. For example,

— Which president served when the country faced its greatest danger?

In game *MEM 6, a question like

— Does this scene take place in the summer?

— What happened just before this photograph was taken?

— What is likely to have happened just after this photograph was taken?

would help you prepare for this kind of memory situation.

Deciding What to Remember

Finally, let's consider *what* information is worth storing in your memory, and what isn't. After all, some information, like telephone numbers, can always be looked up.

Only *you* can decide what is important for you to store in *your* memory. When you do decide to store something, the general principles you've learned in this chapter will be most useful.

Summary of General Principles of Memory

Remember that the most basic principle is to *associate* one thing with another, new things with old.

But of course you will want to remember more than that:

— Organized material is easier to learn.

— Meaningful material is easier to learn.

— Memorizing is easier when you build upon what you already know.

— When possible, store the information to be learned in the form of pictures.

— Whenever you store something in your memory, think about how you will later retrieve it.

— Use a familiar object to remind you of an abstract word or idea.

Applying Principles of Memory to Errands

Suppose there are a number of things you want to do tomorrow in the order listed:

— Call your friend to arrange to play tennis.

— Pay your electricity bill.
— Shop for food.
— Buy "Sports" magazine at newsstand.
— Bring clothes to cleaners.
— Visit friend in hospital.
— Buy gas for car.
— Check on a movie schedule.

Based upon what you have learned in this chapter, you could take the approach of linking the first two errands in an action picture in your mind, then linking the second and third errands in another picture, and so on. You will then have a vivid way to remember your errands. For example, your pictures might be:

— A tennis court whose net is charged with electricity
— A gigantic electric battery with different compartments carved out for dairy products, meat, vegetables, etc.
— A supermarket whose check-out counters are covered by sports magazines.
— Neatly pressed sports magazines wrapped in cellophane and hanging in a cleaning store.
— A cleaning store filled with nurses' uniforms.
— A hospital building in which cars with empty gas tanks are driving in and cars with full gas tanks are driving out.
— Your own car waiting in line for a drive-in movie.

There are, of course, many other areas where you can find your own way to apply the memory principles you've learned to your daily life:

— appointments
— telephone numbers
— addresses
— names of public figures
— learning new words
— remembering train or bus schedules, and so forth.

CHAPTER XIV

APPLICATIONS

In the preceding 13 chapters we have given you activities, puzzles and games to help you improve in various separate skills that make up visual thinking. In some cases we have suggested the practical situations in which you can apply these skills, and even have given some sample situations. Our purpose in this chapter is to help you see the range of possible situations in your life to which you can apply these principles.

Visual thinking does apply to many situations. You must be alert for opportunities to apply what you have learned, and creative in seeing the common elements between puzzle and game situations on the one hand, and everyday problems on the other.

Applications of Visual Thinking on a Trip

Suppose you want to go from New York to San Francisco to visit a friend. There are a large number of decisions you must make, some more important than others, as you plan your trip and actually take it. Let's see where you can apply some of the things you've learned from the activities and games in this book when you make these decisions.

1.   Shall I go by plane?

It's faster to go by plane, but cheaper to go by bus. You must weigh the importance to yourself of time and money.

In playing with the mini-maze in the *Mazes* chapter, you learned that sometimes you get fewer points by taking a longer route from A to B than a shorter route. Think of "getting fewer points" as spending less money, and "taking a longer route" as spending more time. You already have some experience with weighing the importance of two different things, and reaching a decision. Apply this experience as you decide whether to travel by plane or bus.

2.   Which airline should I take?

If you want to stop along the way to visit other friends and relatives, you will use your skills from the *Connections, Mazes* and *Strategy* chapters to plan your route.

3.   Should I check a suitcase?

If you do, you can take more things along. But you risk the airline losing it, your check-in may take longer, and you face delays waiting for it at the baggage claim.

Instead, can you stuff enough of what you want to take into a bag that fits underneath your seat?

Your skills from *Polynominoes, Filling Space, Puzzles* and *Imagine Changes* will help you decide what luggage to take and how to pack.

4.   How should I get from my home to the airport?

You might drive, have a friend drive you, take a cab, take public transportation, etc. Again you must weigh the importance of time and money, as well as convenience in transferring luggage.

Use your skills from *Connections, Mazes* and *Strategy* to plan your route. Keep in mind how you will get back from the airport to your home on your return trip. The "planning ahead" skills from *Strategy* will be useful.

5.   If I decide to drive my car, should I park in short-term or long-term parking?

Again you must weigh the importance of time, money, and convenience.

6.   How shall I find my way around the airport?

Your airline leaves from Terminal B, and you have only been to Terminal A before. But you realize the layouts of each terminal are symmetrical (*Mosaics*), and you quickly find your way around Terminal B.

7.   What shall I do when a four-hour delay of my flight is announced at the airport?

You might try another flight of a different airline (*Strategy, Connections, Mazes*), plan how to fill the time by taking a nap, shopping, reading (*Filling Spaces*). Minimize the number of times you must pass through the airport security check by planning your route to shops, restaurants, restrooms, etc. (*Connections*).

8.   How can I retrieve my luggage quickly?

You tie a yellow ribbon around the handle so you can spot it quickly at the baggage claim area (*Observation*).

9.   How should I choose my seat?

If you think you will be getting up a lot, you ask for an aisle seat (*Strategy, Mazes, Connections*).

As a non-smoker, you want a seat in the non-smoking section. But since smoke drifts, you don't want to be close to the boundary between smoking and non-smoking sections (*Connections*).

10. How shall I pass the time on the flight?

You anticipate (*Strategy*) that you will spend the time (*Filling Spaces*) during the flight by reading a book. You estimate (*Observation*) how much of the flying time you will want to read (perhaps total flight time minus meal time minus bumpy periods) and how fast you read, to decide what book to take.

11. Should I eat before the plane leaves?

You estimate (*Observation*) how hungry you will be before the first meal on the plane, to decide whether to eat before boarding the plane.

12. How else should I prepare myself for the flight?

You anticipate (*Strategy, Imagine Changes*) being at your destination in a new time zone and different climate, as you plan your pre-flight meals, decide how much you will sleep before you leave, and decide on what clothing to wear.

13. Should I rent a head-set?

You recall (*Memory*) from many previous trips that this airline shows uninteresting films, so, expecting another one (*Inductive Logic*), you decline to rent the head set.

14. How do I deal with a brat?

A bored child sitting next to you on the flight has been cranky. You cut out seven shapes from a "This Seat Occupied" cardboard in the pocket of the seat in front of you, and show the child how to make many different pictures with them (*Tangrams*).

15. How can I leave the plane quickly at my destination?

You experience a slow-moving line of people leaving the wide-body airplane at your destination, so you recall the layout of the plane and take a longer but faster path (*Mazes, Memory*) through the plane.

16. How can I recognize the person meeting me?

Your friend is sending his brother, who has never seen you before, to meet you at the airport in San Francisco. In advance (*Strategy*) you and your friend's brother exchange descriptions ("I'm tall, have dark hair, wear glasses, will be wearing a blue shirt and carrying a briefcase in my left hand.") so that out of the stream of passengers and the crowd of people waiting for them, you can recognize each other (*Deductive Logic, Observation*).

Finding Your Own Applications

The above section shows that you do not find everyday life problems neatly labeled, such as "visual thinking applies here, remember principle from game 2 in Memory chapter."

Some situations are very similar to games and puzzles you have already worked on, and others are not so similar. Sometimes the similarity is obvious, sometimes you need some insight to see where and how to apply what you have learned.

Ultimately you must face situations in your life and decide yourself what principles apply.

For example, there has been a power blackout, and one station is damaged. You use what you have learned about mazes, connections, imagining changes and strategy to run lines from nearby stations into the damaged station to provide power, without crossing lines. You find an arrangement that requires the laying of the fewest new cables.

Another example: An auto accident ahead has blocked traffic. By using your memory and maze ability, you turn off before you reach the scene of the accident, and take a route you remember to reach your destination without delay.

Systematic Thinking

In the first chapter we said that the physician, car mechanic and chef all go through the same process: begin with many possibilities, get information, reduce the number of possibilities through deductive logic, get more information, etc., and finally reduce the many possibilities to one. This process is similar to what a physicist or chemist does: runs an experiment, gets information, reaches conclusions, eliminates some possibilities, designs another experiment, etc. You learn this process by playing the games in the Deductive Logic chapter.

Whether you are working with sick people, cars that need repair, food, atomic particles, or pesticides, you will be more successful if you use systematic, organized ways to handle your problems.

In this book, therefore, we have stressed
— a systematic way to build symmetric mosaics.
— a systematic way to reproduce a tangram figure.
— a systematic way to develop a new way to fill space.
— a systematic way to find two identical 2x2 mosaics within a larger mosaic.

You will also benefit from using a systematic approach in your everyday life, even though the specific situations may be very different from the activities, puzzles and games of this book. For example,
— You can't find your car in a large parking lot. You systematically keep track of the lanes of cars you have gone over.
— You are looking for good pieces of fruit in the bin of a food store. You use systematic approaches to keep track of the pieces of fruit you have already examined.

Here are some of the advantages when you use systematic approaches:
— you have a plan to guide your actions.
— you keep track of what you've already done.
— you can discover your mistakes and not repeat them.
— you use your resources (time, materials) wisely.
— you see more alternatives.
— you make decisions more easily.
— you avoid being influenced by others who know less about the problem than you do.
— you anticipate and avoid future problems.

More Application Opportunities

In the rest of this chapter we give you some more examples of direct and indirect applications of the activities, games and puzzles of this book to practical problems. The examples are organized by chapter.

Mosaics

Copying Drawings

You can copy a drawing by using the grid and mosaic concepts. Suppose you want to copy a drawing made from mosaics, like that in Fig. 1. Set up a scale, such as 1:2. This means that each tile will be twice as high and as wide as the tile it replaces (Fig. 2).

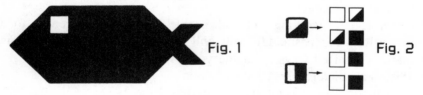

Fig. 1   Fig. 2

Fig. 3 shows an enlargement made this way.

Fig. 3

You can apply a similar technique to other drawings not made from mosaics. Imagine (or lightly draw in) grid lines that divide it into small and simple-to-copy squares (Figs. 4a,4b). Think of each square as a tile that you now place on a new grid. To copy the original drawing larger or smaller than the original drawing, or in a different perspective, make your new grid larger or smaller or in a different perspective (Figs. 4c,4d). This technique is one that master artists use, too.

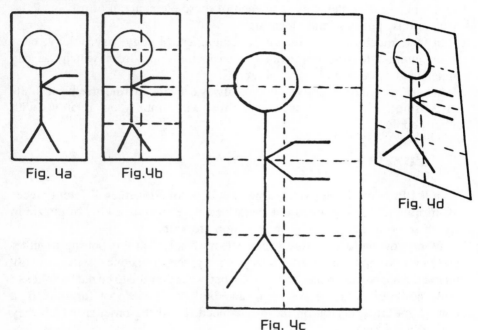

Fig. 4a   Fig.4b

Fig. 4d

Fig. 4c

Symmetry

In the Mosaics chapter you learned about the concept of symmetry. You can apply this concept to a practical problem when you take an object apart. Some of its pieces may be symmetric, and others not. Fig. 5 shows a nonsymmetric nut. While you might put it back either oriented from left to right or from right to left, it will only fit tightly one of these ways.

Always check whether a piece you remove is symmetric. If it is not, you must replace it the same way it was before.

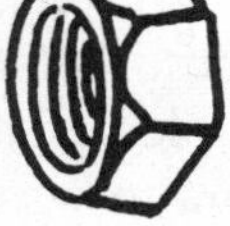

Fig. 5

More General Life Applications

You have seen that complicated designs and drawings of objects can be built up from very simple building blocks. Complicated life situations, too, can often be broken up into simple building blocks or elements.

In the field of chemistry, for example, we know that everything on our earth (people, trees, rocks, and the earth itself) is made up of some combination of just 104 elements, and each of these elements in turn is made up of neutrons, protons, and electrons.

In fact, much of our research in economics, biology, psychology, etc., is an attempt to find out what the basic units are from which we can understand more complicated situations.

In our everyday life, too, we are always trying to find the basic units (friendship, trust, love, respect, etc.) that will simplify our relations with other people.

Puzzles

In the Puzzles chapter you learned about putting together different pieces of information. We pointed out that a detective story is a kind of puzzle in which some of the pieces of information are verbal.

When you build a model airplane from a kit, you are putting together pieces according to the instructions you are given. Someone else has already planned what pieces are needed and in what order they are to be put together.

If, however, you are designing and building a piece of furniture or a house, you must decide on the pieces needed and the order in which they are put together.

Tangrams

An archeologist who finds some fragments of a jar and tries to reconstruct it uses skills from Puzzles and Tangrams.

Filling Spaces

You can use the ideas of tesselation whenever you need to use space efficiently. For example,
— You want to design a parking lot so that it held the most cars possible.
— You are cutting out many copies of the same shape from a piece of wood or cloth, you would want to waste as little material as possible.
— In packing for a trip you would want to get as much into your suitcase

as possible.

Suppose you were cutting many sleeves for garments from a large piece of cloth. Each sleeve is the shape shown in Fig. 6.

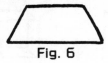

Fig. 6

Fig. 7a shows a layout that is very wasteful. Fig. 7b shows a layout that is less wasteful. Can you do better?

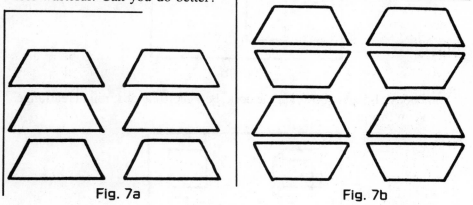

Fig. 7a   **Fig. 7b**

Fig. 7c shows a maximally efficient layout. It is based upon the idea you met earlier that any four-sided polygon can be tesselated.

Layout of Desk

Suppose your desktop contained an in-basket, out-basket, stapler, writing pad, and telephone. You might arrange these things as shown in Fig. 8a.

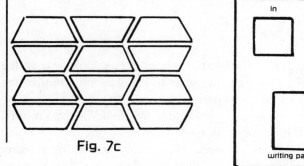

Fig. 7c

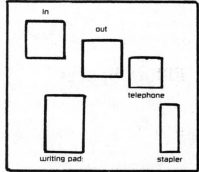

Fig. 8a

If you need more space, you might place the in-basket on top of the out-basket, and make the other changes shown in Fig. 8b.

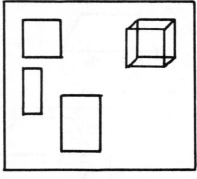

Fig. 8b

Somebody else who took over the desk, being left-handed, might rearrange it as shown in Fig. 8c.

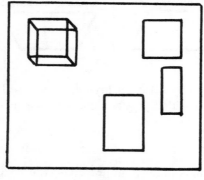

Fig. 8c

Layout of Living Area

Everyone has the problem of living somewhere. Let's look now at the specific problem of efficiently organizing your living area: how to plan the layout of the furniture in a house or apartment.

To begin with, let's say you have a rectangular area to divide into rooms, and furniture to arrange within these rooms.

First decide who is living in this area: how many adults, how many children. Decide what each does during the day: work, stay home, go to school.

Suppose your total living area is represented by a piece of graph paper 8 x 20, and your pieces of furniture and their sizes are the following:

6 chairs	1 x 1 (boxes of graph paper)
3 armchairs	1 x 1
1 sofa	1 x 3
4 beds	2 x 4
2 cupboards	2 x 4
2 low cabinets	2 x 2
3 tables	2 x 3

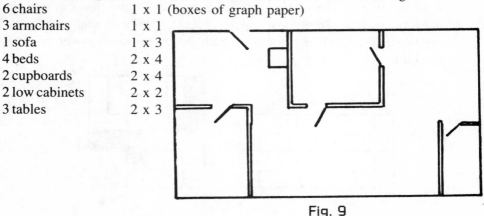

Fig. 9

Now, plan out on the graph paper how the living space will be divided into rooms, and how the furniture will be arranged in each room (Fig. 9). Do this before you read further.

Check whether you've taken into account these considerations in your planning:

— Are there doors leading to each room?
— In getting from one room to another, is it necessary to go through a third room? Is this convenient?
— Does each room have a window?
— Is there enough space to move around in each room?
— Does any piece of furniture block access to a door or to something else?
— Are there closets in the rooms that should have them?

This list may suggest still other considerations to you.

Think through the daily routine of each person who would live in this apartment or house. Trace the routes people would walk, point by point. Could some trips be eliminated by a different layout of rooms and/or of furniture?

Start again from the beginning, with a different size living area, a different set of people, and a different set of furniture. Have several of your friends go through the same kind of planning separately. Then compare the layouts each of you has come up with. Ask yourself the questions given above. Discuss with the others why you did what you did. From the others' points of view you can learn what factors you didn't think of. You will see how some things are important for some people and not for others. You may also exchange creative ideas for saving space, for example, placing one bed on top of another.

Fabric Cutting

In the Filling Spaces chapter, we mentioned laying out a design on a piece of fabric in a tesselated way in order to cut it with minimal waste. If the fabric is colored differently on each side, you can flip over the design as you tesselate it (Fig. 10).

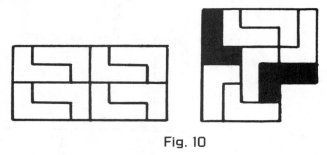

Fig. 10

Parking Lots

Fig. 11 shows four different possible arrangements of cars in a parking lot. Can you design a different way that fits more cars into the same space, and allows them to get in and out easily?

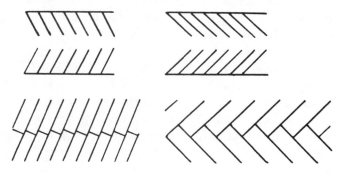

Fig. 11

Miscellaneous Situations in which to Apply Tesselation
— Plan house lots in village
— Farms on plot of land
— Packing items in a suitcase
— Packing suitcases into the trunk of a car

Mazes

You can apply the skills you learned in connecting dots in the fewest lines possible to the problem of finding the shortest route on a map, and to a salesperson to find a route that passes through all the stops that need to be made.

Schematic and technical drawings provide a shorthand language for communicating a lot of information at a glance. By building and solving mazes you increase your ability to understand the information presented in schematic and technical drawings. Mazes develop your patience and determination.

Observation

You can apply your skills from this chapter in many aspects of office work: proofreading, filing, estimating margins for a business letter, etc.

Connections

Highway Interchanges

Topology is involved in designing interchanges, so that roads connect smoothly, allowing people to turn off where they want to (Fig. 12). Maze ability is important in highway design too.

Fig. 12

Toll Bridges

In both the San Francisco Bay Area and the New York City area, planners have used topology to eliminate tolls in one direction on tunnels and bridges. This speeds up traffic.

At the time the new system was put into effect, the tolls were doubled. Since most drivers make round trips eventually (for example, to and from Manhattan), the total amount of money collected under the new system was the same as before. Fig. 13 shows the New York City situation.

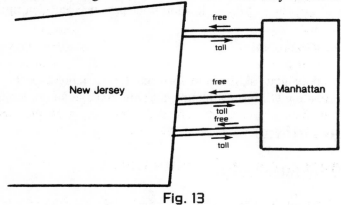

Fig. 13

An Airport

An airport area is usually divided into two regions: one for passengers who have been through the security check, and another for those who haven't.

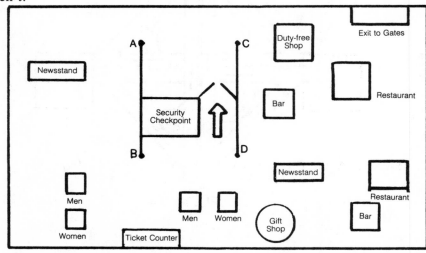

Fig. 14

Fig. 14 shows an airport area.

a.   Extend the lines AB and CD so that they completely divide the area into two regions, with passage between the two regions only at the checkpoint.

             Each region should contain the following:

Before Checkpoint	After Checkpoint
Restaurant	Restaurant
Bar	Bar
Men's room	Men's room
Women's room	Women's room
Newsstand	Newsstand
Ticket counter	Duty-free shop
Gift shop	Exit to gates

             A solution is given at the end of the chapter.

b.   See if you could redesign the airport area to make it simpler and more efficient. You may want to reread the tesselation chapter section on designing an apartment before you start.

Connections and Deduction

Three houses, A, B and C must each be connected with gas, electricity and water, by lines that do not cross each other. (Fig. 15). Can this be arranged?

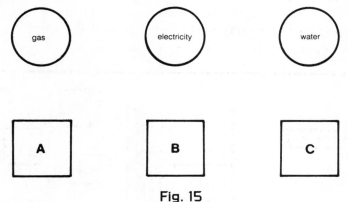

Fig. 15

Suppose A and B are already connected, as in Fig. 16.

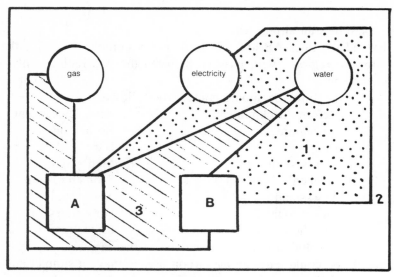

Fig. 16

This means that the entire area has been divided into three regions. Where could house C be located?

— In region 1, it would be cut off from gas.
— In region 2, it would be cut off from water.
— In region 3, it would be cut off from electricity.

By combining topology and deductive logic, we see that it is impossible for the three houses to each be connected up with the three utilities by separate lines that do not cross.

Solution

Page
175

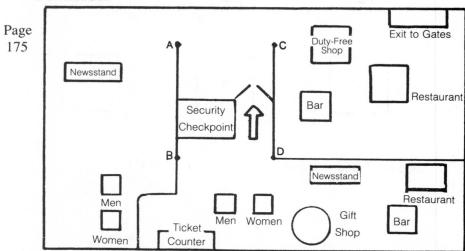